Handbook
of
Knots

by
Raoul Graumont

SOUVENIR PRESS

First published in the U.S.A. by
Cornell Maritime Press

First British Edition published 1973 by
Souvenir Press Ltd, 95 Mortimer Street, London W1N 8HP

ISBN 0 285 62115 7

Printed in Great Britain by
Fletcher & Son Ltd, Norwich

ACKNOWLEDGMENTS

In preparing this volume, it has been the author's good fortune to have the valuable aid and material assistance of the following men in the U.S. Navy: R. J. Rouis, CBM, U.S.N.; S. E. Franks, CBM, U.S.N.; C. H. "Tex" Collings, CBM, U.S.N.; R. B. Ausve, BM 1/c, U.S.N. I wish to acknowledge with thanks the generous cooperation they have so willingly extended.

To Mr. John Hensel, with whom I collaborated in the preparation of the *Encyclopedia of Knots and Fancy Rope Work,* goes much of the credit for the material contained in this volume.

I am also indebted to Mr. S. H. Hieatt and Dr. P. E. Minter for submitting valuable knot designs.

Grateful acknowledgment is also made to Mr. Don Selchow for his painstaking efforts in producing the excellent photographs used in this book.

RAOUL GRAUMONT

PREFACE

Down through the ages men have found fascinating interest in the development of practical and ornamental knot work. Ever since Neolithic man tied a stick to a stone for his first axe, knots have played an important part in the life of man. So it can be truthfully stated that the formation of useful knots with rope or cordage of some kind was one of man's earliest and most essential tools. The use of knot work was widespread, and a high degree of skill in the making of rope and the development of knots was achieved long before the dawn of recorded history.

The art of knot work reached a high stage of perfection among the early Egyptian sailors, and knots were used in building bridges and rigging ships in Egypt and Greece. The reef knot was well known in ancient Greece and Rome, as may be seen in many surviving works of classical art. It was used to ornament the handles of vessels, and almost always appeared on the staff of Mercury. It was reproduced in many pieces of sculpture and also on the girdles of Roman Vestals. The ancients called it the Knot of Hercules.

Ornamental knotting has been employed for ceremonial purposes in Japan since early times when it was apparently a subject of devoted study. It was also used in Europe during the last days of Knighthood in the Middle Ages, when a wide variety of patterns appeared as decorative inscriptions on shields and badges of Heraldry.

Although rope and knot work has been used for thousands of years by nearly all races of the globe, it was not until the comparatively recent period of long sea voyages in sailing ships that certain types of intricate knot work were developed. During this period of marlinespike seamanship the Cape Horn sailormen devoted many hours of their leisure time to tying and combining different basic weaves which were formed into beautiful rose designs and ornamental weaves that became their pride and joy.

Sennit braiding is another interesting art. It was and still is utilized by Mexican cowboys for making leather and horsehair whips and sombrero chin straps. The cowboys of western America have also used it to some extent in braiding saddle ornaments and lariats. It reached the peak of its development in France during the last century when this beautiful work was utilized in making harness, riding crops, quirts, belts and many other useful articles.

Coxcombing has also come into vogue in recent years. It is used for ornamental effect in dressing up hand rails, bucket handles and numerous other objects that have attracted the skill of modern seamen.

Turk's Heads were probably the most popular of all the old-time ties that have been handed down to the present generation. They retain their popularity because they are undoubtedly the most attractive and adaptable of all ties for decorative purposes. They lend themselves to a wide variety of weaves that can be used to cover suitable objects such as stanchions and railings. They present a beautiful and uniform appearance.

Fiber rope splicing has been practiced almost since rope was first used, for, without some form of splice, rope itself is at times almost useless. If rope is used with the proper kind of splice, however, it has almost unlimited possibilities in the performance of countless jobs.

The numerous uses of the various types of fiber rope splices are so well known as to need little elaboration. Suffice it to say that rope splicing is practiced in all ships and shipyards for rigging and other purposes. It is also employed extensively where rope is used for power transmission when leather belts or other means are unsuitable. It is difficult to overestimate the importance of this type of rope work, since splicing is used in so many ways in our jobs in daily life. The ability to turn in a rapid and secure splice will sometimes save an almost hopeless situation in an emergency.

The inclusion in this book of knot work relating to trades, industries and professions will fill an urgent need for a convenient reference text to meet the ever-growing demands of numerous maritime and vocational training schools, trades and industries, and of professional people in every walk of life who have occasion to use knots in their work.

The work itself will not only serve many practical purposes but will also lead to the mastery of an artistic and interesting hobby. At the same time, the student will derive a deep sense of satisfaction from knowing how to make a knot properly and how to apply it to the correct situation.

Once a sound basic knowledge of the various ties has been acquired, the student will discover fascinating possibilities for creative development of advanced knot work. The success with which he masters the more advanced knot work depends to a great extent upon personal initiative and a genuine determination to learn the subject step by step.

In this HANDBOOK OF KNOTS, it is my sincere desire to give the beginner and the advanced student a complete selection of all the common types of knot work that both will find useful in the practice of any one of more than fifty trades, industries or professions. Also included are basic knots and weaves that form the framework of all categories of general knot work, such as Sennit Braiding, Ornamental Designs, End Rope Knots, Coxcombs, Turk's Heads, Lashings, Bends, Hitches, Bowlines, Sheepshanks, Splices and various other forms of ties.

The text has been carefully prepared and every effort has been made to explain in sufficient detail the procedure of construction of the various examples, which are clearly illustrated with photographs of each operation.

It need hardly be emphasized that the student should make every effort for his own interest to master the methods used in tying the simple basic knots, and should familiarize himself with each step of the succeeding operations before attempting to execute a more intricate piece of work. He should also learn thoroughly the many ways in which the various combinations of knots are used to form other knots. Only in this way can he hope to understand the different methods of tying and combining intricate designs in fancy creations such as those explained in *The Encyclopedia of Knots and Fancy Rope Work*.

In the preparation of these knots, any rope or line can be used that will best serve the purpose for which the knots are intended.

In a special index in the back of this volume are listed the knots that are of particular interest and value to each of these professions or hobbies: Merchant seamen, Naval and Coast Guard sailors, yachtsmen, power boatmen, Scouts, Sea Scouts and Mariners, Camp Fire Girls, cowboys, farmers, riggers, trappers, hunters, lumberjacks, tailors, florists, grocery men, carpenters, fishermen, linemen, millers, longshoremen, packers, surgeons, surveyors, teamsters, butchers, electricians, magicians, firemen and circus men, campers, draymen, forest rangers, prospectors, mountain climbers, truck drivers, weavers, divers, well diggers, steeplejacks, tree surgeons, mattress makers, net makers, brick masons, hoisters, soldiers, stationers, artists, designers, decorators and leather workers.

It is hoped that the material contained here will serve to bring the ageless lore of knot work to everyone who has an interest in this most fascinating and useful subject.

RAOUL GRAUMONT

TABLE OF CONTENTS

	PREFACE	vii
1	HITCHES	3
2	HITCH AND TOGGLE TIES	6
3	HITCHES	9
4	STOPPER HITCHES AND TURK'S HEADS	13
5	BENDS	19
6	SHEEPSHANKS	20
7	BOWLINES	22
8	SIMPLE KNOTS	25
9	SIMPLE KNOTS	29
10	SIMPLE KNOTS	33
11	SIMPLE KNOTS AND MATS	35
12	MATS AND ORNAMENTAL KNOTS	37
13	ORNAMENTAL KNOTS	40
14	ORNAMENTAL AND TRICK KNOTS	42
15	GENERAL KNOTS	45
16	GENERAL KNOTS AND HITCHES	49
17	SENNIT BRAIDING	50
18	END ROPE KNOTS	55
19	END ROPE KNOTS AND SPLICES	59
20	EYE AND CUT SPLICES	63
21	SHORT AND LONG SPLICES	67
22	SPLICES, GROMMETS AND WHIPPINGS	70
23	WHIPPINGS AND SEIZINGS	77
24	GENERAL KNOTS AND TIES	80

25	MISCELLANEOUS KNOTS	83
26	MISCELLANEOUS HITCHES	87
27	MISCELLANEOUS KNOTS AND BRAIDS	88
28	GENERAL KNOT WORK	92
29	MISCELLANEOUS HITCHES AND KNOTS	95
30	BARREL SLINGS	98
31	PACKAGE AND PACK MULE TIES	100
32	ROPE COILS AND GASKETS	103
33	ROPE SHORTENINGS AND SLINGS	106
34	ROPE LADDER MAKING	109
35	GENERAL KNOT WORK	111
36	GENERAL KNOT WORK	115
37	BOATSWAIN'S CHAIR AND LASHINGS	118
38	METHODS OF SECURING HAWSERS	123
39	A STAGE SLING AND BELAYING PIN TIES	124
40	VARIOUS TYPES OF POLE LASHINGS	128
41	ROPE POINTING, FLEMISH AND SPINDLE EYES	130
42	NET MAKING AND MESHING	134
43	HAMMOCK CLEWS AND GROMMET EYELETS	138
44	STEPS IN MAKING A SEA BAG	141
45	STITCHES USED IN SEWING CANVAS	144
46	BLOCKS AND TACKLES	148
47	BLOCKS AND TACKLES	151
	TERMINOLOGY	155
	CARE AND HANDLING OF ROPE	158
	GLOSSARY	160
	INDEX OF KNOTS	183
	INDEX OF KNOTS BY JOB AND HOBBY	191

Handbook of Knots

Plate 1—HITCHES

Fig. 1: The *Single Half Hitch* is the simplest hitch there is and forms the foundation for many important knots. It is very seldom used alone, except when the end is seized to the standing part.

Fig. 2: *Two Half Hitches* serve a variety of purposes such as securing the end of a rope to a ring, spar or any other object. Their construction can be easily followed by observing the illustration.

Fig. 3: The *Sailor's Hitches* shown here are tied in the reverse manner to the previous method. Hitches such as these are useful as mooring ties for small boats.

Fig. 4: The *Clove Hitch on the Standing Part* is used in the Navy to tie neckerchiefs. Its formation is simple and easy to follow.

Fig. 5: The *Reverse Clove Hitch on the Standing Part* is tied in the opposite manner to the previous method. This form of tie has very few uses.

Fig. 6: The *Lark's Head* or *Cow Hitch* is serviceable when an equal tension is applied on both standing parts, but is valueless when a strain comes on one part only. It is used on baggage tags or whenever a parcel is bound with the bight of a line. It can be tied in the middle of a line when the ends are inaccessible, merely by passing a bight through the ring and then flipping it back over the ring on to the standing part.

Fig. 7: The *Lark's Head Stoppered* shows an overhand knot used as a stopper for the lark's head. Knots such as this may be used to advantage when securing the end of a line to an anchor ring or any other similar object.

Fig. 8: The *Crossed Lark's Head* has the ends of the line coming out on opposite sides as the picture illus-

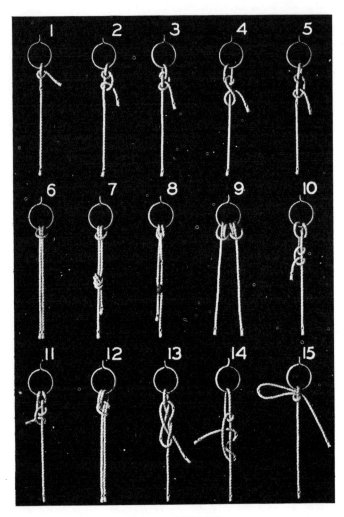

Plate 1—HITCHES

4

trates, instead of through the bight as for the two previous methods. It is shown stoppered with a seizing.

Fig. 9: The *Treble Lark's Head* is tied by forming a reverse bight with the ends passed through from underneath. A half hitch is then formed on each side in the manner indicated.

Fig. 10: The *Backhanded Sailor's Hitches,* first method, are another of the various ways of attaching a line to a ring. They are made by passing an end of the line around the inside of a ring, then under its own standing part and back around the ring again, and are finished off with two half hitches around the standing part.

Fig. 11: The *Backhanded Sailor's Hitches,* second method, are tied in practically the same manner as in the previous method, except that the bottom hitch is tied in reverse, or the opposite way from the first style of construction.

Fig. 12: The *Double Lark's Head* shown here is begun by first tying the sailor's hitches illustrated in Fig. 3. Continue by doubling the top part back around the ring and then follow the standing part down through the hitch, which will complete the double form of this tie as illustrated.

Fig. 13: The *Capstan Knot* is a variation of the figure-of-eight knot. It is used mainly as a temporary fastening, but is otherwise unreliable. Its construction can be easily followed from the illustration.

Fig. 14: The *Midshipman's Hitch* is more commonly known to yachtsmen and fishermen as a *Topsail Sheet Bend*, acquiring its name from the use to which it is put. It consists of a half hitch made with the end around the standing part, plus a round turn inside half hitch just below it. This form of tie will not shake free when the strain on it is relaxed, hence its use for securing the end of a topsail sheet to the clew cringle in the sail. It is also used by tree climbers as a form of safety tie on their taut lines to adjust the proper height of their swing boards. See Plate 36, Fig. 342 for a more dependable variation of this tie.

Fig. 15: The *Slip Hitch* is made by first passing the line a full turn around the object it is to be attached to. Then a full turn is taken around the standing part, and the bight of the end is tucked through the knot in the manner illustrated. It may be used as a temporary fastening where it is necessary to untie the end quickly, but it is not safe under a continued strain.

Plate 2—HITCH AND TOGGLE TIES

Fig. 16: The *Gunner's Prolong* or *Delay Knot* is more commonly known by gunners themselves as a delay knot. It is nothing more than a simple carrick bend with the upper loop run through two rings.

Fig. 17: The *Latigo Tie* is used by horsemen for securing the strap or saddle girth to the cinch ring. The top ring represents the saddle ring and the bottom ring represents the cinch ring.

Fig. 18: The *Halter* or *Manger Tie* is the method most commonly used for tying horses to the mangers in their stalls.

Fig. 19: The *Hackamore Tie* is another form of knot that is used for the same purpose. When the slip eye is released, the tie will automatically come undone.

Fig. 20: The *Buoy Hitch* can be used for any purpose that requires a safe temporary tie that can instantly be undone by pulling on the end of the line forming the slip eye, after the line has been eased. Its method of construction can easily be followed from the illustration.

6

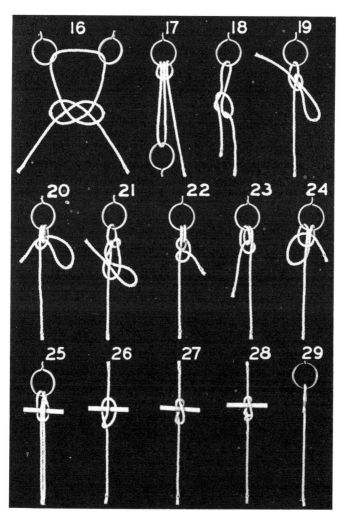

Plate 2—HITCH AND TOGGLE TIES

7

Fig. 21: The *Mogul Bend* or *Sampan Hitch* shown here is used to moor skiffs and to lower such objects as small tools, so that the line can be drawn up again.

Fig. 22: The *Fisherman's Bend* shown here follows the orthodox method of construction frequently employed on yachts. The bend is formed in the following manner. First, take two round turns around the object to which it is to be attached. Then pass the working end around and under the standing part and through the round turn forming a half hitch. Follow with another half hitch to make it secure. If the tension is not continuous it is better to seize the end to the standing part, since the knot is likely to shake itself free if the end is not secured.

Fig. 23: The *Anchor Bend* which is also known as a *Fisherman's Bend* is a remarkable knot because of its simplicity and great strength. It will not slip, chafe, or jam. After withstanding severe tension, it can easily be untied when the strain on the line is eased.

Fig. 24: The *Ring Hitch* is of simple construction and can be followed easily from the illustration.

Fig. 25: The *Lark's Head with Toggle* can be released instantly by withdrawing the toggle. It is unnecessary to have access to the ends of the rope to form this knot. It is effective, however, only when there is constant tension on both standing parts, and even then should be used only temporarily.

Fig. 26: The *Boat Knot* is used for mooring small boats. When the toggle is withdrawn, the knot instantly comes adrift. It is similar to a marlinespike hitch, except that a toggle or pin is used instead of a marlinespike.

Fig. 27: The *Figure-of-Eight with Toggle* has the toggle to resist added tension.

Fig. 28: The *Stevedore's Knot with Toggle* employs the same principle as the knot in Fig. 27.

Fig. 29: The *Seized Loop* is a temporary fastening made by simply passing the end of the line through a ring or around a spar and seizing it to the standing part. It is not advisable to use this loop if anything heavy is to be attached to the standing part, as it is likely to carry away.

Plate 3—HITCHES

Fig. 30: The *Clove Hitch* or *Ratline Hitch*, which has a number of uses, is frequently employed to secure a line to a stanchion or spar or to fasten the ratlines to the shrouds, hence its name. This very useful knot is not only easily tied, but is also quite secure when made on a spar. Its method of construction is quite easy to follow and needs no elaboration.

Fig. 31: The *Magnus Hitch* resembles the inside rolling hitch, but differs in that it has one overlapping turn which goes from the left side completely across the knot to the right side. It is formed by first making a round turn on the spar, then crossing over the two top turns and going completely around the spar again. The end is disposed of by putting it under the outside turn. This brings both ends of the line, or the working part and the standing part, out on opposite sides of the cross turn on top.

Fig. 32: The *Timber Hitch* is useful in securing a rope temporarily and quickly to a spar or piece of timber. It does not hold well unless it is kept taut. The twist should be in the same direction as the lay of the rope, which may easily be remembered by always thinking of it as "dogged" with the lay.

Fig. 33: The *Killick Hitch* is an adaptation of the timber hitch with an additional twist taken with the

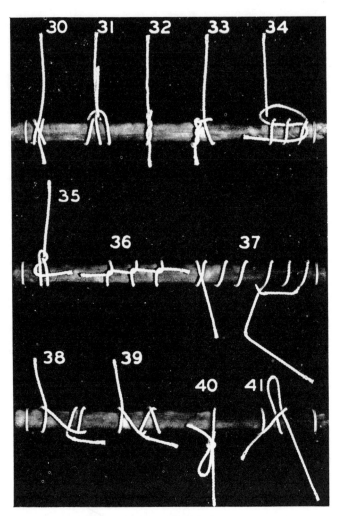

Plate 3—HITCHES

working end of the rope after a half hitch has been taken with the standing part around the object it is to be attached to. It is a good way to secure a large stone or other object when a temporary anchor is needed. It is also used for certain lifting purposes.

Fig. 34: The *Topsail Halyard Bend* in this illustration is tied in the orthodox manner. This method is never used on merchant ships, but is sometimes employed on yachts. It is formed by first taking three round turns around a spar; next, the working end is brought back around the standing part and passed back under all three turns, then back over the last two and under the first turn again.

Fig. 35: The *Studding-Sail Boom Hitch* or *Stunsail Halyard Bend* is made by taking a round turn around the spar. Then bring the end around the standing part and back under the round turn and its own part. It is then tucked over the first part and under the second part in the opposite direction, as illustrated. This knot was used on the studding-sail booms of sailing vessels. It can also be formed by making the round turn on the opposite side of the standing part, with the working part of the line tucked from right to left to finish the knot.

Fig. 36: The *Marline* or *Hammock Hitch* consists of a number of overhand or thumb knots (as many as necessary) made consecutively around an object, such as a yard, boom, stanchion. It has many uses, such as "marling down" the nettles or foxes when pointing a rope. Sails, bundles, or packages may be kept in a neat roll by marling them down with light rope. The marline is also a very useful hitch to apply when setting up wind dodgers to the jackstays.

Fig. 37: A *Reef Pennant Hitch* is used to secure the reef cringle to the boom. A reef pennant is a rope that passes through a comb cleat on the end of the boom, through the reef cringle on the sail, then down through a comb cleat on the opposite side of the boom.

Fig. 38: The *Inside Rolling Hitch* is tied as follows: Take a turn around the spar and then bring the line over the standing part and cross it to the opposite side of the spar. Continue by taking a round turn on the inside of the cross turn which will bring the working part out on the inside of the knot. This is the correct way the turns should be taken in bending a line to a spar. This is a valuable knot ashore or afloat, because it can be tied around a smooth surface without slipping. It can also be untied very easily. Another important feature of this knot is that it may be applied either at a right angle to the spar or parallel with it.

Fig. 39: The *Orthodox Rolling Hitch,* sometimes called *Outside Rolling Hitch,* is tied by taking a turn around the spar, then bringing the line to the opposite side of the spar and making two turns, bringing the line back under both parts, as illustrated. This is the method that is employed to bend a line to a rope.

Fig. 40: The *Slip Halter Hitch* is formed by putting the end of the line about the object or spar to which it is to be fastened, and then tying an overhand knot around the standing part. The end is then tucked back through the body of the knot. This hitch can be easily untied by simply pulling the end.

Fig. 41: The *Slip Clove Hitch* is a variation of the ordinary clove hitch. It is made the same way except that on the last tuck the bight, rather than the end, is placed under the turn. This is a handy knot, as it can be slipped and untied quickly.

Plate 4—STOPPER HITCHES AND TURK'S HEADS

Fig. 42: The *Stopper Hitch* is formed by making a half hitch with the end of the line around the spar, rope, chain, or whatever it is to be used on. Then the end is backed around the object in the opposite direction from which the strain is to be applied. In use, the part hanging down should lead to the right, almost parallel to the object upon which it is fastened, and should be made fast to a stationary object. After the turns have been dogged around the rope or spar, the end is held in the hand. The author has found that in actual practice these backing turns should always be taken with the lay of the rope (if it is put on a rope), as it tends to hold better due to the added cross-friction. The regular stopper hitch shown in Fig. 44 is superior to this one, because the added turn gives it greater holding power, and if a heavy weight is to be suspended, it is much safer to use the stopper with more than one turn.

Fig. 43: The *Two Half Hitch Stopper Hitch* is used for the same purpose as the stopper hitch in Fig. 42, although made somewhat differently. Every person who uses a stopper knot has his own pet method of applying it. Some prefer the rolling hitch or one of the various other types. Experimentation has shown that, if applied to a rope, two half hitches are the most satisfactory, because the knot can still be cast free easily even when a great amount of tension is applied to it. The regular stopper hitch shown in Fig. 44 usually jams when a heavy weight is placed on it. Tension is applied to the knot in the direction indicated by the arrow.

Fig. 44: The *Regular Stopper Hitch* is the most widely used of all stoppers. This hitch will hold even when the rope is wet or greasy because the heavier the load, the tighter the knot becomes. In this case, as in all stoppers,

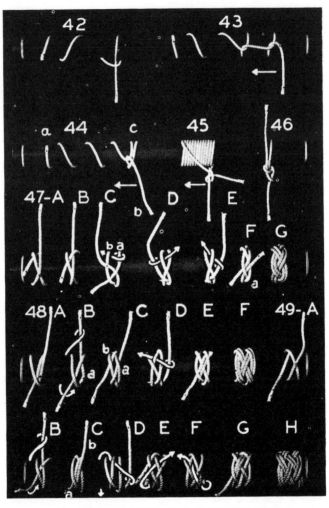

Plate 4—STOPPER HITCHES AND TURK'S HEADS

the end made fast to the bitts or other object is marked *b*, and the end held in the hand is marked *a*. End *a* was left short in the illustration for obvious reasons, but in reality it is a little longer. First, take a turn around the rope, forming a half hitch. Next, take another turn around the rope and inside the original half hitch. The end should then be at point *c*, from where it is taken back and dogged with the lay. Notice the difference between this hitch and the hitch shown in Fig. 42. Tension is applied to the knot in the direction shown by the arrow.

Fig. 45: The *Lifting* or *Well Pipe Hitch* will also bear a strain parallel to the object to which it is fastened. It is used to secure the guy ropes of a circus tent to stakes driven into the ground or, as the name indicates, to hold a well pipe being lowered into the earth. It is formed by first taking a number of round turns about the object, as many as desired (the more the better). Then when enough have been put on, the end is brought across the top of the turns, and two half hitches are made around the standing part. Tension is applied to the knot in the direction shown by the arrow.

Fig. 46: The *Weaver's Hitch* is really a bowline, but it is made like a weaver's knot or a sheet bend. This is a very useful method of hitching a line to a spar or other object, because it will not give and is easily untied.

Fig. 47 A: *Three-Strand Turk's Head*, first stage is represented in this illustration. Now turn your work to B.

B: This shows the second stage of the work, with the free end taken from the right, up and between the two turns.

C: The turn *a* is to be pulled under the turn *b*, as shown by the drawn line.

D: The knot will now look as in D. The turn on the

right-hand side was pushed to the left and under the left-hand turn. The moving end is now passed as shown by the arrow.

E: This shows how the Turk's head should look after the tuck has been placed as described in D. The moving part is now taken from the right to the left, under and up through the center as the drawn line indicates.

F: The work is again turned, to position F. At this position, *a* indicates the movement just executed in E. The working end was on the right-hand side, and has been passed through the right to the left. The Turk's head is now complete, and all that is necessary is to follow the standing end with the moving end. However, be sure to watch that the passes taken to double the Turk's head do not cross each other. After following around twice, the Turk's head appears as in G.

G: This shows the Turk's head as it looks when finished, if the directions have been carefully followed. As a rule three passes are made to complete most forms of Turk's heads, however only two passes are used here in order to clarify the illustrations.

Fig. 48 A: *Four-Strand Turk's Head.*

B: Notice that at *a* the moving part goes under both turns, instead of over and under.

C: The working end is then brought completely around the spar on the left-hand side, to the left of all the turns which have already been taken, and is brought over *b* and under *a*, which will lock these strands.

D: The work is again turned until position D is reached. (Some of the turns may slip out of place as the knot is being worked on, and should be adjusted until they resemble the illustration.) At this point the working end is put over, under, and over as the drawn line indicates. This is the final tuck to be made in the Turk's head, and the work when turned appears as in E.

16

E: The moving end here follows the beginning as in the three-strand Turk's head, until two or three passes are made. The ends are then put underneath the Turk's head before it is drawn up; after it has been worked tight around the spar, the ends are cut off close.

F: The four-strand Turk's head, when finished appears as illustrated.

Fig. 49 A: Beginning a *Five-Strand Turk's Head.* The first two movements (A and B) are in this case the same as for the three-strand Turk's head.

C: The end is brought completely around the spar on the left-hand side of the knot, to the left of all the turns, as in C of the four-strand Turk's head just described. In this illustration, *a* is the standing part, and *b* is the moving part. The moving part is brought over and under, following strand *a*, to the right-hand side.

D: The work at this stage is turned to correspond with the illustration D, the drawn line indicating where the strand is to be put over, under, and over.

E: The work is now turned over, to correspond with E. At this point the two parallel strands are split and the moving strand is passed, as the drawn line shows.

F: The work is again turned until this position is reached. The moving part is then passed between the parallel strands under, over, under, and over for the last tuck to complete the Turk's head as shown in G.

G: The moving end at this point follows the original beginning until two or three passes have been made.

H: The Turk's head is now complete and appears as in H. The ends are placed underneath and the work drawn taut. Turk's Heads have many uses.

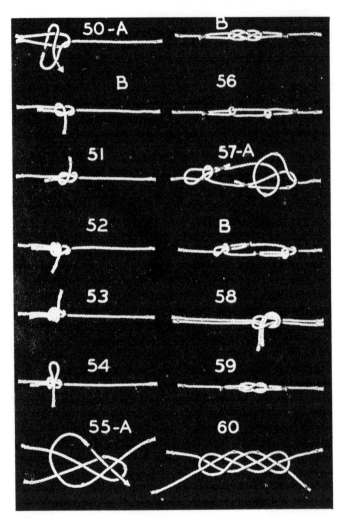

Plate 5—BENDS

Plate 5—BENDS

Fig. 50 A: The *Right-Handed Sheet* or *Becket Bend* is also known as a *Single Bend, Common Bend, Simple Bend* and *Swab Hitch*. It was once in very common use as a means of bending a sheet to the clew of a sail. When used for joining ropes of different sizes it holds much better than the reef knot. It is made by forming a bight in one rope and a half hitch with the other rope as the drawn line indicates. Weavers use this knot when a thread in a loom breaks. It has also been used for centuries in the making of nets.

B: Shows the finished sheet bend.

Fig. 51: The *Left-Handed Sheet* or *Becket Bend* is tied in the reverse manner to the ordinary sheet bend, with the ends coming out on opposite sides, as illustrated.

Fig. 52: The *Double Sheet Bend* is formed in the same way as the sheet bend, but with an additional turn around the bight and under its own part. This is a very good knot to use when bending together lines of two different sizes. Always use the larger line for the bight or loop.

Fig. 53: The *Triple Sheet* or *Becket Bend* is formed with three turns around the bight, otherwise it is the same form of tie as the other methods.

Fig. 54: The *Slip Sheet Bend* can be released instantly by pulling on the end of the slippery hitch.

Fig. 55 A: The *Double Carrick Bend* has the line laid out as shown to form the pattern of the knot. The drawn line shows how the knot is closed up.

B: This shows the completed carrick bend with the ends seized.

Fig. 56: The *Reeving Line* or *Single Marriage Bend* is formed with a hitch on each side as illustrated, but it is not safe unless both ends are well seized to standing parts.

Fig. 57 A: The *Bowline Splicing Bend* has a bowline tie in the bight of each end. This shows one end of the bowline tie opened up.

B: This shows the tie completed.

Fig. 58: The *Sheet Bend on a Bight* is formed the same way as the regular sheet bend, but with two ends of the line instead of one. This knot is employed when two tackles are used.

Fig. 59: The *Half Carrick Bend* is tied by forming a cross in one end and leaving the other end open.

Fig. 60: The *Prolonged Carrick Bend* has an additional cross worked in on each side of the regular bend.

Plate 6—SHEEPSHANKS

Fig. 61 A: The *Ordinary Sheepshank* is used for shortening a rope. The rope is first laid out to form two bights. A half hitch is then formed on each end of the bights as shown on the left side of this illustration.

B: This shows the finished sheepshank.

Fig. 62: The *Man O' War Sheepshank* has a Spanish knot tied in the middle of the bights.

Fig. 63: The *Cat Shank* is a form of rope shortening in which the bights are seized with overhand knots on each side as illustrated.

Fig. 64: The *Dog Shank* has an overhand knot seizing on both ends of the shortening.

Fig. 65: The *Knotted Sheepshank*, in which the strain is borne more equally by the different parts of the rope, is an improved variation of the dog shank.

Fig. 66: The *Sheet Bend Sheepshank* represents another method of knotting the ends of a sheepshank. The ends are passed around the bights, and then through their own parts.

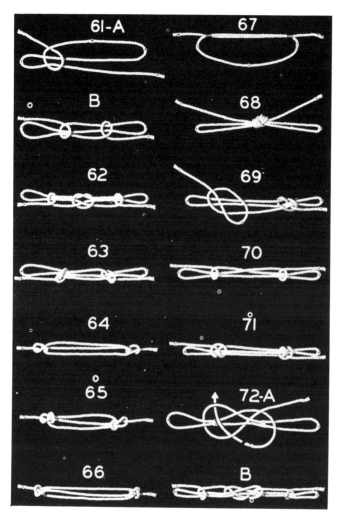

Plate 6—SHEEPSHANKS

21

Fig. 67: The *Seized Loop Shortening* has seizings on each end as shown.

Fig. 68: The *Overhand Shortening* is formed by tying an overhand knot in the middle of two bights, which have been made as though for a sheepshank.

Fig. 69: The *Marline Hitch Sheepshank* has marline hitches formed on both bights as illustrated.

Fig. 70: The *Sheepshank with the Middle Crossed* is a novel method of tying the ordinary sheepshank.

Fig. 71: The *Sheepshank with Ends Double-Hitched* is a secure way to finish off a sheepshank.

Fig. 72 A: The *Interlaced Sheepshank* has the knot in the middle of the bights as shown here. The drawn line indicates how it is closed.

B: This shows the completed sheepshank.

Plate 7—BOWLINES

Fig. 73 A: The *Bowline* is sometimes called the king of knots, and is the most useful way to form a loop in the end of a rope. Though simple in construction, it never slips or jams; and after severe tension has been applied to it, a simple push of the finger will loosen it enough to untie. The bowline is really a sheet bend with a loop, but is made somewhat differently. To make it, take the standing part in the left hand. The end, held in the right hand, is then laid on top of the standing part and grasped with the thumb and the index finger, the thumb being underneath. Next it is twisted up and away from you until Fig. 73 A is reached. Then the end is put around the standing part and down again through the loop, as the line shows.

B: This represents the finished bowline.

Fig. 74 A: The *French Bowline,* or the *Double Chaise*

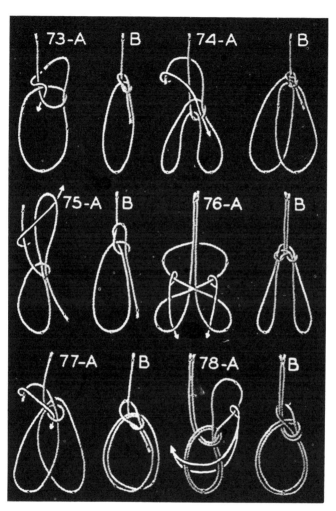

Plate 7—BOWLINES

23

de Calfat, (Double Caulker's Chair) is superior to the ordinary bowline as a sling because it allows a man to use both hands. It is especially advisable to use this bowline when lowering a man into a smoke-filled hold or anywhere there is danger of his losing consciousness as it is impossible for a man to drop out of this type of sling. The formation of the French bowline is illustrated in its first stage in Fig. 74 A.

B: This shows the finished French bowline as ordinarily used. A man sits in one of the loops, passing the other one about his chest and back under the armpits. The man's weight in one loop draws the other loop under the arms taut.

Fig. 75 A: The *Ring* or *Stopper Bowline* is made when you have a coil of rope and only want to use some of the end. To make the rope fast to something, the ring bowline is utilized, being formed as follows: First, the end is rove through a ring as much as desired; next, the end on the right side of the ring is taken in the right hand and formed into a bight; the end on the left-hand side is taken in the left hand, and a half hitch is put over the bight in the right hand, as in Fig. 75 A; then the free end on the top is rove through the bight, as the line shows.

B: This shows the finished ring bowline. It can also be used on the cover draw lines under the belly of a lifeboat.

Fig. 76 A: The *Spanish Bowline* may be tied in many different ways. But this method is the simplest to illustrate. It is made with the bight of a rope, and laid out as shown. The two bights on each side on top are then put through the loops on the bottom, as indicated by the drawn line.

B: This shows the Spanish bowline after the bights have been passed through the loops, and the knot drawn up tight. The knot pictured here can be used as a form of chair to sit in, although the French bowline is preferable for this purpose.

Fig. 77 A: The *Portuguese Bowline* at first glance appears to be the same as the French bowline, but is in reality slightly different, as the second turn, instead of going through the gooseneck, passes over the top of it.

B: This represents the Portuguese bowline in its finished form. It can be used for the same purpose as the French bowline, but the latter is to be preferred.

Fig. 78 A: The *Bowline on the Bight* is formed on the bight of a line when the ends are inaccessible. To tie this knot, the bight of a rope is laid out to correspond with the illustration. It will be noted that the first step conforms to the beginning of the ordinary bowline. The drawn line indicates how the bight is passed around the bottom of the knot, then up again around the standing part. To the novice, this knot may seem quite mysterious and difficult, but it is really very simple to master. Many years ago, mischievous boys would tie this knot in the reins of a horse while the driver was engaged elsewhere. When he returned, he usually found it necessary to unhitch the reins from the horse's head in order to straighten them out and untie the knot.

B: This shows the finished bowline.

Plate 8—SIMPLE KNOTS

Fig. 79 A: The *Stevedore's Knot,* opened up in this photograph to illustrate its method of construction, is used mainly to prevent the end of a rope from unreeving.

B: Back view of the same knot pulled up taut.

C: Front view that illustrates the appearance of the knot on the opposite side.

25

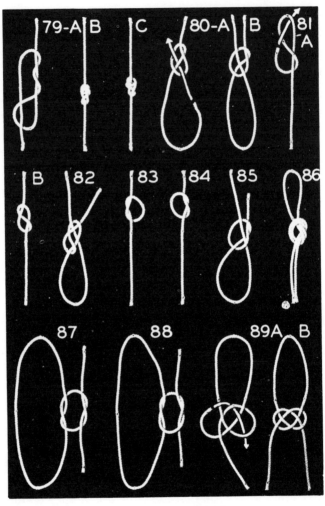

Plate 8—SIMPLE KNOTS

Fig. 80 A: The *Crossed Running Knot* is a running eye that gives added friction. It is seldom used. The line is laid out as shown in the first step and the drawn in line indicates how the opposite end is passed through the body of the knot to complete the operation.

B: As the same knot will appear when completed.

Fig. 81 A: The *Figure-of-Eight Knot* is often used as a stopper knot because it does not jam and opens quite easily. It has few uses as a practical knot, but is popular for ornamental work as it makes a very decorative tie and is simple in design.

B: The same knot as it appears when finished.

Fig. 82: Shows a *Running Figure-of-Eight* with the standing part passed through the body of the knot in the manner indicated.

Fig. 83: Shows an *Overhand* or *Thumb Knot*. It is the most common form of tie in existence, being used by almost everyone for many different purposes. It is often used as a stopper knot to prevent a rope from running out of a block or falling through an opening. However it should be used in this manner only as a temporary tie, because the knot has a tendency to jam hard under strain and is difficult to untie afterward. Furthermore, it should never be used in preference to the proper form of whipping or pointing to prevent the end of a rope from unraveling or fraying. A rope with an overhand knot tied in its body should never be used without first untying the knot, as a rope with a knot in it possesses less than one-half the breaking strength of an unknotted rope.

Fig. 84: The *Overhand Knot* shown here represents the opposite method of tying this form of knot.

Fig. 85: The *Running Overhand Knot* is tied the same as the ordinary overhand knot, except that one free end forms a loop by passing through the body of the knot.

Fig. 86: The *Openhand Eye Knot* or *Binder's Loop* is a

common method of forming a loop in the end of a line. It is sometimes used for securing packages, but half hitches are preferable in most instances when a tie of this type is required, as the tie shown in this illustration jams hard and is difficult to untie.

Fig. 87: The *Granny Knot* is the most dangerous form of knot in existence, as it is often tied by mistake while attempting to tie the more secure square knot. It should never be used for any purpose as it is completely untrustworthy and either slips or jams when subject to tension or strain. The beginner should study closely the characteristics of this knot and then compare it with the square knot that is shown in the next illustration. It will be noticed that the working ends of the line lead out in the opposite manner to the standing part after the knot is formed, whereas in the square knot the working ends lead out in the same manner as the standing part.

Fig. 88: The *Square* or *Reef Knot* is the oldest and most useful method of joining two pieces of cordage. It is used for a large variety of purposes such as tying up bundles or other objects, or to tie the reef points in a sail. However, it should never be used if the ropes are of different sizes or materials, as it jams hard under tension. Do not join two hawsers together by this method. The reef knot is formed by tying an overhand knot first, then another overhand knot is formed in the opposite manner and on top of the first one as the picture illustrates.

Fig. 89 A: The *Sailor's Breastplate* shown here represents a double carrick bend tied in the end of a bight. It is made with an underhand loop crossed under, by reversing the strand pointing toward the right as the picture illustrates, and then passing it underneath the body of the knot to the left side. It is then closed up with the strand from the left side as indicated in the photograph by the drawn in line.

B: The knot as shown here represents the completed operation. This knot is useless and is made mainly as an ornamental version of the double carrick bend.

Plate 9—SIMPLE KNOTS

Fig. 90: A *Running Noose* or *Slippery Hitch* such as that shown here with a thumb knot on one end, is used extensively for commercial purposes as a package tie. It is formed by tying an overhand knot around a slip eye.

Fig. 91: A *Flemish Eye Knot* is tied by forming a double figure-of-eight in the end of an eye. It is seldom used.

Fig. 92 A: The *Hackamore, Theodore* or *Indian Bridle Knot* was first used by the Plains Indians to decorate horsehair bridles. Later a variation of this tie known as the hackamore halter was used on the western frontier as a temporary rope bridle and bit for breaking wild and unruly horses. It is tied by forming two bights in the manner shown. The bight on the left is then pulled up over the top part.

B: With the bight lying in place over the top of the knot as illustrated here, the drawn in line indicates the next move. The inside line on the left is grasped and pulled under the standing part or free end of the line on the right, then down through to the outside. This operation will take up the slack from other parts of the knot and at the same time form its own bight as the knot is pulled up in place.

C: This shows the completed knot turned right side up or in the opposite direction.

Fig. 93 A: The *Two-Strand Carrick Diamond Knot* is made by first forming a sailor's breastplate with one end of the line coming out on the inside of the loop and the other end coming out on the outside of the knot as shown.

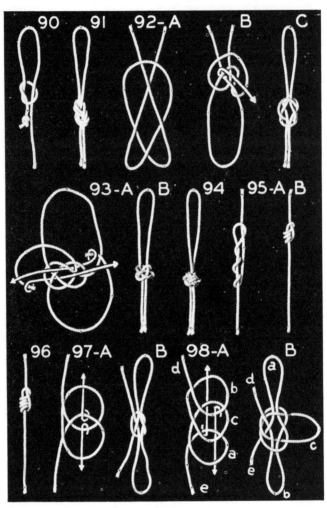

Plate 9—SIMPLE KNOTS

Next pass both strands underneath and out through the middle of the knot as illustrated by the drawn in lines. Continue by pulling the knot taut while, at the same time, each strand is worked up and into place uniformly.

B: This shows the knot as it should look when pulled up properly. It is a very attractive and popular knot and is widely used for decorative purposes.

Fig. 94: The *Two-Strand Carrick Diamond Knot* shown here is doubled, or has two passes instead of one.

Fig. 95 A: The *Three-Fold Knot* is shown here opened up to clarify its method of construction.

B: This shows the same knot pulled taut. It can be used to weight the end of a line.

Fig. 96: The *Four-Fold Knot* has an additional pass. Otherwise it is tied in the same manner as the three-fold knot.

Fig. 97 A: The *Single Jury Mast* or *Spanish Knot* is begun by forming two loops with one overlapping the other in the manner shown, then the bights are pulled through as the drawn in lines indicate.

B: This shows the completed knot. Knots such as this are often used in the body of sheepshanks.

Fig. 98 A: The *Double Jury Mast Knot* is used for rigging a jury mast. Bights *a, b* and *c* form a means of attaching supports to the mast. The center of the knot is slipped over the masthead, and stays are bent to the three bights by using sheet bends. The ends *d* and *e* are joined with a bowline, with one of the ends serving as a fourth stay, in order to complete the staying of the jury mast. The knot is formed by three overlapping loops as shown. The loops are pulled through as the drawn in lines indicate, placing bight *a* on the left, and bight *b* on the right. Then bight *c* is pulled out on top.

B: Illustrates the completed knot as it appears when the bights have been pulled through to the outside.

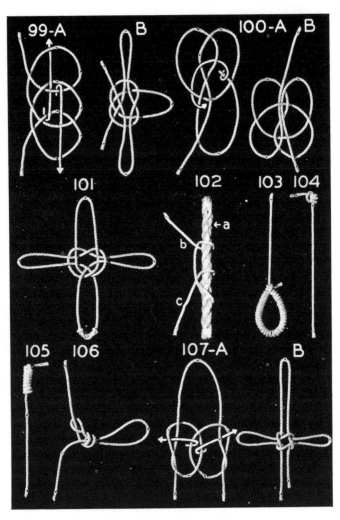

Plate 10—SIMPLE KNOTS

32

Plate 10—SIMPLE KNOTS

Fig. 99 A: The *Jury Mast* or *Masthead Knot* is similar to the double jury mast knot and can be used for the same purpose. These two knots can also be used for jar slings, the four bights serving as handles and the center of the knot being placed over the neck of the jar or pitcher. Form three loops as illustrated, each loop overlapping the other; then pull the bights through as the drawn in lines indicate to form outside bights as in the jury mast knot, at the same time pull the top part out to complete the knot. To form the bottom bight, join the ends together with a bowline.

B: Shows the knot as it appears when finished with the bights pulled through to the outside.

Fig. 100 A: The *Japanese Knot* is a simple form of ornamental decoration. To start the knot, lay the loops out in the manner shown, the drawn in line indicating how the design is closed with the working end of the line.

B: The finished knot as shown here represents the two loops joined together to complete the operation.

Fig. 101: The *Double Pitcher Knot* is constructed in the same manner as the double jury mast knot except that the bottom bight is spliced together as illustrated. All such knots as these can be used for jar, jug or pitcher slings.

Fig. 102: The *Roofers Hitch* is used by a roofer or painter to lower himself down a roof. The standing part is indicated by *a; b* is the point where the knot is grasped by the hands; while *c* is the part that is made fast around the body.

Fig. 103: The *Terminal Knot* is used for weighting the end of a heaving line. To start the operation make an eye in the end of the rope. Then take the end and wind it around the eye until the standing part is reached. The turns are now drawn taut, then worked up snug by adjusting the eye from the standing end of the line. The end is seized to the standing part to finish off.

Fig. 104: The *Multiple Overhand Stopper Knot* is tied by taking a series of turns in a loop or in other words by the same principle used in tying an overhand knot, but with two additional turns made before pulling taut. It is used in this fashion as a stopper knot.

Fig. 105: The *Heaving Line Knot* is often used in place of the monkey fist to weight the end of a heaving line. However, it is considered poor seamanship to use the knot aboard ship in this manner, and for that reason it is relegated chiefly to the use of landlubbers. First form a bight on the end of a rope. Next take the end of the line and wind it around toward the end of the bight until the desired number of turns have been reached. The end is then put through the eye of the bight, and the standing part is pulled to draw the eye down taut on the knot and bring the turns up snugly in place.

Fig. 106: The *Lifeboat Draw* or *Slip Knot* is used in the draw lines under the belly of a lifeboat to make the cover fast. It is tied by laying out a bight and then taking two turns around the body with the working end of the line, which is rove through the eye at the opposite end, as indicated, to complete the operation.

Fig. 107 A: The *Shamrock Knot* is a simple ornamental knot of exceptional beauty, used extensively for decorative purposes. It is tied by forming two interlocking overhand knots with the ends in reverse to each other as the picture illustrates. The drawn in lines show how each inside part is then pulled through the body of the two overhand knots to form the outside bights.

B: This represents the completed knot. This knot looks more attractive when doubled.

34

Plate 11—SIMPLE KNOTS AND MATS

Fig. 108 A: The *Single Fisherman's Knot* is ordinarily used to tie gut, which is less likely to slip when tied with this form of knot than when joined with a reef knot or sheet bend. It is tied with the underhand loop on the left overlapping the underhand loop on the right in the manner shown. The bight is then pulled through as the drawn in line indicates.

B: Illustrates the knot after the operation has been completed. This knot is often called an Englishman's, true lover's or waterman's knot.

Fig. 109 A: The *Tom Fool's Knot* or *Arizona Handcuff Hitches*, also known as a *Conjurer's Knot*, is said to have been used as a rope handcuff in the early days of the West. It can also be used as a jar or pitcher sling. It is tied by forming a loop in the manner shown, with one part of the line crossing over and the other part crossing under the knot. The bights are then pulled through as indicated.

B: The completed knot is shown here.

Fig. 110: The *Crabber's Eye Knot* is tied in the reverse manner of the crossed running knot on Plate 8, Fig. 80. Before the knot is pulled taut it can be used as a running knot, as part *a* will function in the same manner as an ordinary slip knot. When part *b* is hauled upon, the knot jams in the form of a sheet bend, thereby making it a secure tie under strain.

Fig. 111 A: In the *Chinese Square Mat* the bight on the left interlaces the bight on the right. The end of the line from the left bight is formed into another bight and passed through in the manner indicated.

B: This shows the step just referred to, completed, with the bight passed through the body of the knot. The drawn in line indicates how the weave is now closed up.

C: This illustrates the completed operation. This form

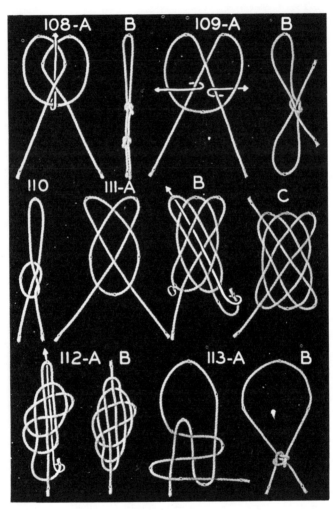

Plate 11—SIMPLE KNOTS AND MATS

of knot work can be expanded as far as desired by using the same key over and over again before closing the weave with the last pass.

Fig. 112 A: The *Triangle Mat* is begun by forming two bights in the same manner as in the preceding method. However, the bights are formed each time by the end of the line on the left, which first goes under the bottom part of the previous bight that was tucked. Otherwise the method of operation is the same as in the Chinese Mat. It will be noted that this method alternates the working parts after each move, whereas the former method is constructed with the same working part. This mat likewise can be expanded by using a repetition of the same key and it can also be doubled by making two passes if desired, which similarly applies to all other mats and ornamental weaves.

B: This shows the mat as it appears when completed.

Fig. 113 A: The *Japanese Crown* or *Success Knot* is a very beautiful knot for ornamental purposes and has been used in this manner by the Orientals since ancient times. The method of its construction can be followed easily by observing the interlaced bights in the open illustration. It is better for the student to try to commit patterns like this to memory after tracing them a few times. In this way it will be easy to duplicate the designs without constantly referring to the illustrations.

B: This illustrates how the knot appears when the weave has been completed.

Plate 12—MATS AND ORNAMENTAL KNOTS

Fig. 114 A: The *Napoleon Bend Mat Weave* is shown here with the line laid out in the form of an overhand knot and the bights pulled out and crossed over as indicated to start the weave.

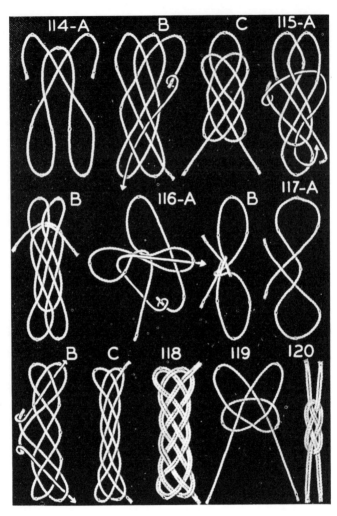

Plate 12—MATS AND ORNAMENTAL KNOTS

B: The bight on the right side is now crossed over on top of the bight on the left, and the working part of the line is next passed through the weave by going under the bight from the left and over the bight from the right. The drawn in line indicates how the weave is closed.

C: This shows the mat completed. It can be double or triple passed if a large mat is desired. This type of weave makes an attractive ornamental decoration and is often used as a floor mat when woven with manila rope.

Fig. 115 A: The *Square Mat* is begun by arranging the line as indicated. The drawn in lines show how the weave is closed up.

B: This illustration shows the same mat as it appears when completed. It can also be enlarged by making additional passes.

Fig. 116 A: The *Two-Leaf Dragonfly* is formed in the manner shown; the end is passed over and around the two bottom parts and back out by its own part as the drawn line indicates.

B: This pictures the knot as it looks when finished. It is one of the oldest forms of ornamental decoration among the Orientals.

Fig. 117 A: The *Queen Anne Mat Weave* is begun by laying the line out in the position shown here.

B: Next form bights with both working ends, one bight going over, and the other going under, its own part in the manner indicated. The bights are now passed through each eye that was previously formed in order to enlarge the weave. After this has been done, the operation will appear as illustrated. The drawn lines indicate how the ends are passed through to complete the weave.

C: This shows the same weave as it looks when finished. By using the same key as described above, the mat can be extended to any size desired before closing the mat with the last pass.

Fig. 118: In the *Double Queen Anne Mat* shown here, the lines are doubled by an additional pass. Otherwise it is the same weave as in the previous method.

Fig. 119: The *Three-Strand Inverted Turk's Head* is an ordinary three-strand Turk's head as shown on Plate 4, Fig. 47 with the bights pulled out and lying flat.

Fig. 120: The *Wake Knot* is useful as an ornamental knot. It was used for that purpose on shields and badges of heraldry during the declining days of knighthood. It is really a double carrick bend design.

Plate 13—ORNAMENTAL KNOTS

Fig. 121 A: The *Three-Leaf Dragonfly Knot* has many uses in ornamental knotting, and should be thoroughly mastered. The work is first laid out as shown in this illustration, and a bight is pulled through the loop as the arrow indicates. If this knot is first tied on a table or some other flat surface until it is learned, it may then be tied in the hand much more rapidly.

B: Following Fig. 121 A, the work appears as shown. The end is then put through the loop as indicated by the arrow.

C: Next, the end is again put through as the drawn line indicates.

D: After Fig. 121 C has been completed, and all the slack has been drawn out, the work appears as in this illustration.

Fig. 122 A: The *Two-Leaf Chinese Temple Knot* is made in the same general way as the three-leaf Chinese temple knot, except that two bights are formed instead of three. Part *b* is crossed over part *a* and under part *c*, part *c* is crossed over part *b* and under part *a*, part *a* is crossed over part *c* and under part *b*.

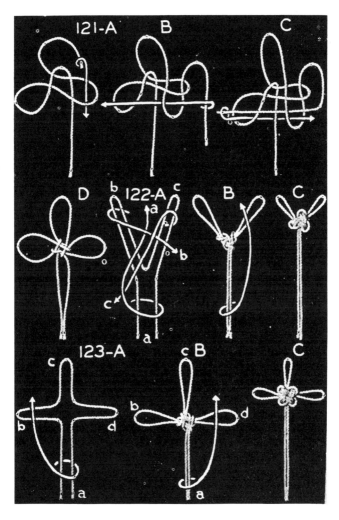

Plate 13—ORNAMENTAL KNOTS

B: This shows the knot after the last of the previous tucks has been completed and the slack drawn out. The ends are then crowned again in the same manner as in Fig. 122 A or the opposite way as indicated here.

C: The finished knot is shown here after both loops have been adjusted to the same size. The picture illustrates the knot from the front side.

Fig. 123 A: The *Three-Leaf Chinese Temple Knot* is a useful knot in ornamental work and surprisingly simple to make. The cord is first laid out on a table, as shown in the illustration. Ends *a* are laid over bight *b*, bight *b* is laid over bight *c*, bight *c* is laid over bight *d*, and bight *d* is then put through the loops left by ends *a* when they were brought up. This final tuck is made in the same manner as in Fig. 122 A.

B: After the operation just described, the work appears as in this figure. The next step is to repeat this procedure, and tie another crown on top of the knot just made. This time crowning to the left rather than to the right. The drawn line indicates the next step.

C: After the crown has been made, the finished knot appears as shown. This illustrates the knot from the front side.

Plate 14—ORNAMENTAL AND TRICK KNOTS

Fig. 124 A: The *Brief Knot* is made as follows: A reef knot is first made, with a loop on top of the knot, as shown in this illustration.

B: The knot is then turned upside down and a second reef knot made, with the loop coming through the body of the knot. The ends are then brought up and put through the body of the first reef knot as indicated by the arrows.

C: After the step just explained has been completed,

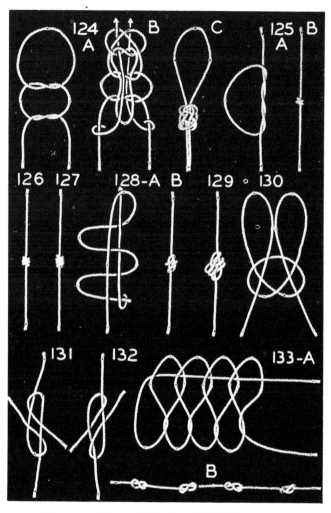

Plate 14—ORNAMENTAL AND TRICK KNOTS

43

the knot is turned again so that the loop faces up. When all the slack has been taken out of it, it will appear as in this illustration.

Fig. 125 A: The *Two-Fold Blood, Bullion,* or *Manifold Knot* is used when it is desired to shorten a small rope, or increase its diameter to prevent it from passing through the eye of a hole. The knot is formed by merely tying a series of turns through a loop, and then pulling taut. This illustration shows the knot opened up.

B: This represents the knot pulled up to complete the operation.

Fig. 126: The *Three-Fold Blood Knot* is tied as in the preceding method, except that it has three turns instead of two.

Fig. 127: The *Four-Fold Blood Knot* is tied like the two previous knots, but with four turns.

Fig. 128 A: The *Double-Figure-of-Eight Knot* is shown open here, the drawn line indicating how the knot is closed.

B: Illustrates how it looks when finished and drawn up.

Fig. 129: The *Three-Fold Figure-of-Eight Knot* is tied with three turns instead of two.

Fig. 130: *Handcuff Hitches* are said to have been used instead of iron shackles on prisoners in the old days of sailing ships; hence the name. When this knot has been made, the two loops are placed over the wrists and drawn tight. The two ends are then reef-knotted together. If the reader makes this knot and places it on someone's wrists, no doubt will be left in his mind as to its security.

Fig. 131: The *Double Becket Tie* when formed with the ends of two lines and drawn taut, assumes the appearance of two becket bends.

Fig. 132: The *Grass* or *Strap Knot* is a good method to use for tying strops or straw together. It is exactly the reverse of the double becket tie.

Fig. 133 A: The *Figure-of-Eight Trick Knot* is an interesting design. This illustration shows how the end of the line is passed through the open figure-of-eights.

B: This indicates how the design appears after the line has been pulled through.

Plate 15—GENERAL KNOTS

Fig. 134: The *Lineman's Knot* is tied by first forming a bight, then putting a half hitch around the bight from both sides with the free ends of the rope with the hitches interlacing. Mountain climbers call this a butterfly knot. It is used by the middle man on the line of a three-man climbing team.

Fig. 135: The *Davenport Brothers' Trick Knot* is so called because it was used by these celebrated performers in doing a rope trick on the stage. It is tied by joining two lines together with an overhand knot. Then two running knots are made just below the overhand knot in the manner illustrated.

Fig. 136: The *Honda* or *Hondo Knot in Lariat* is shown as it is used in cowboy's lariats. It is made by first forming an eye through an overhand knot. Another overhand knot is then tied to keep the eye from pulling out.

Fig. 137 A: The *Weaver's Knot* is actually nothing more than a common sheet bend. The following illustrations show how this knot is made by weavers when a thread in a loom breaks. When there is a "smash" as the weavers say (when all the threads in the warp break) they are knotted together as follows: two threads are taken between the thumb and the index finger of the left hand, and placed in the position shown in this illustration. The drawn line indicates the next step.

B: After the end has been brought around as shown in

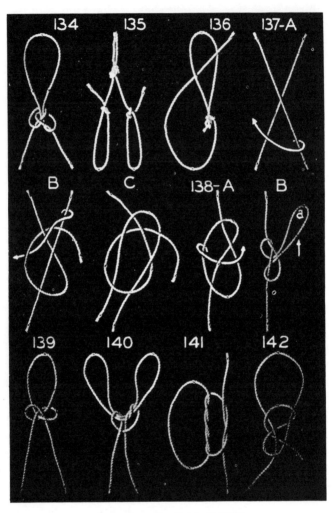

Plate 15—GENERAL KNOTS

the preceding illustration, the other end is then brought down and through the bight as shown by the drawn line.

C: After this tuck has been made, the knot is now finished, and all that remains is to draw out the slack. The weaver's knot is sometimes called the smallest of all knots.

Fig. 138 A: The *Man-Harness* or *Artillery Knot* is useful when a number of men have to haul a heavy object, such as a cannon or other piece of artillery, by means of a single line or rope. First the rope is placed in the position shown in this illustration; then the bight is pulled in the direction shown by the arrow in order to finish tying the knot.

B: After the bight has been pulled through as directed, the knot will appear as shown. Make as many knots as there are men. Each man puts his arm through loop *a*, and places it over his shoulder. The strain is then exerted in the direction of the arrow, each man adding his share to the line.

Fig. 139: The *Teamster's Hitch* is nothing more than a single carrick bend tied in a loop. It is a useful and secure knot and does not jam under a strain.

Fig. 140: A *Rigger's Hitch* is used primarily as a sling such as those used for hoisting purposes. The manner in which the hitch is made is so clearly illustrated that no explanation is necessary.

Fig. 141: The *Surgeon's Knot* is a double overhand knot with a reverse overhand knot on top. The ends come out parallel with the standing part. This knot is used by surgeons in operations.

Fig. 142: The *Mattress-Maker's Knot* is used to tie tufts together in the making of mattresses. Its simple formation needs no explanation.

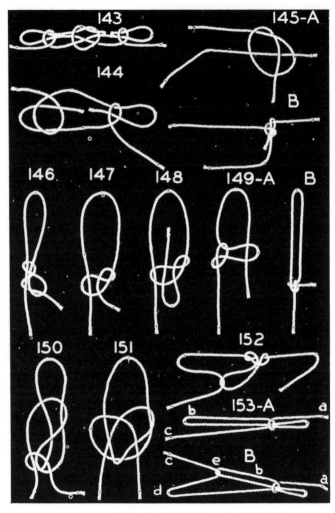

Plate 16—GENERAL KNOTS AND HITCHES

Plate 16—GENERAL KNOTS AND HITCHES

Fig. 143: A *Cut Sheepshank with a Spanish Knot* is used to attach a line to a fixed object and is frequently used when a man desires to lower himself from aloft without leaving a line hanging. The sheepshank is secured to the fixed object, as a spar, and the outside part is cut, as shown, just above the Spanish knot. Such a tie as this is sufficiently strong to support a man, and the lower part of the knot and line can be shaken out and hauled down.

Fig. 144: A *Cut Sheepshank* such as that shown may be used for the same purpose as the cut sheepshank with a Spanish knot, shown in Fig. 143. In the cut sheepshank the middle part is cut, instead of the outside part as is the case when a Spanish knot is used. The lower end of this line can also be shaken out and hauled down.

Fig. 145 A: The *Becket Seizing* is a method used to secure two lines together for the purpose of hauling them aloft or lowering away. It is also used for attaching paint brushes, hammers or any other light objects to the end of a line that is to be hauled up to men working aloft on smoke stacks, masts, etc. Any kind of working tool that is used can of course be lowered in the same manner. First form a marlinespike hitch, then pass the line or other object through the knot in the manner illustrated here. The knot is now drawn taut to secure the tie.

B: This shows how the seizing will appear when pulled taut into a becket.

Fig. 146: The *Ralph Hitch* is a handy way of making a line fast, and is easily made as the picture clearly shows.

Fig. 147: The *Trapper's Hitch* is a form of running figure-of-eight that is easily duplicated.

Fig. 148: The *Trapper's Hitch with Bow* has a bow or slip eye that can be released instantly by pulling on the end of the line.

Fig. 149 A: The *Camper's Hitch* is handy for certain uses around camp. Its method of construction consists of an eye that is hitched around the base as illustrated; the end of the line is then run through the eye and the knot is pulled taut.

B: This shows the finished knot as it appears after the slack has been pulled out of the eye.

Fig. 150: The *Farmer's Loop* shown here is formed with two interlacing bights.

Fig. 151: The *Farmer's Loop*, second method, forms a secure loop which can be tied without access to either end of the rope, and can easily be untied after being drawn tight.

Fig. 152: The *Drayman's* or *Truckman's Hitch* is used for securing the tops of loads on drays, trucks, etc.

Fig. 153 A: The *Dutchman* is a knot generally used in the circus and by truckmen. A very useful design, it forms a strong purchase and may be utilized when a block and tackle is not available. By using this knot, the amount of tension which can be applied to part *a* increases 75%. In use, part *a* leads from the object to be fastened down. The bights, *b*, are next taken, and a half hitch passed over them, as shown in this illustration. End *c* is then passed through an eye or hook, or around some object. This tie may have an extra half hitch placed over the two bights for added security.

B: After end *c* has been passed around the object indicated at *d*, it is passed through the lower end of bight *b*, at point *e* and made fast to complete the operation.

Plate 17—SENNIT BRAIDING

Fig. 154: The *Three-Strand Sennit* is begun with strand *a* on the left and *b* and *c* on the right. Start with *c*, lead it down over and across *b* to the left side; then lead *a* down over and across *c* to the right side. This method is repeated until the desired length of braid has been completed. The beginner will find it easier to learn if he letters the strands as they are in the illustrations.

Fig. 155: The *Three-Strand Double Sennit* is braided in the same manner as the single method in Fig. 154, and double strands *a*, *b* and *c* worked accordingly.

Fig. 156: The *Four-Strand Round Sennit* is begun by leading strand *a* down around and in back, then under *d* and over *c* toward the left side. Next lead strand *d* down around and in back, then under *b* and over *a* toward the right side and so on. This method is repeated as many times as necessary until the desired length of braid has been reached. The braids can be started from either side. Always keep left and right hand groups of strands divided and in their proper places.

Fig. 157: The *Four-Strand Single Flat* or *English Sennit* is begun in the following manner: Lead strand *b* under *d* and over *c* to the opposite side. Next lead strand *a* over *b* to the opposite side. Continue by leading strand *d* under *c* and over *a*. The same moves are now repeated with each strand until the braid is finished. When braiding with an even number of strands in a flat braid, the outside strand on one side has to be started under, and the outside strand on the opposite side has to be started over. With an odd number of strands the outside strands on both sides have to be started over, then under, etc.

Fig. 158: The *Five-Strand Single Flat* or *English Sennit,* is begun with the strands divided 3-2. Lead strand *a* across the front, then over *b* and under *c* toward the opposite side. Next lead strand *e* across the front, then over *d* and under *a* toward the opposite side and so on. The rule to follow is over one, then under one, across the front towards the opposite side, and vice versa.

Fig. 159: The *Seven-Strand French Sennit* is begun with

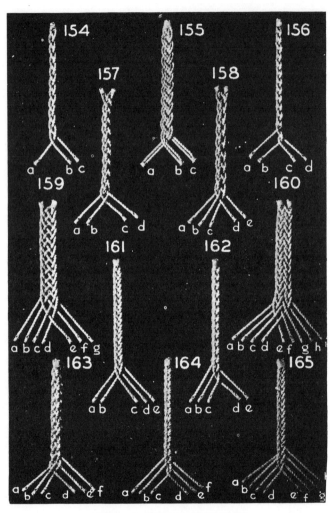

Plate 17—SENNIT BRAIDING

the strands divided 4-3. Start with strand *a* across the front, then over *b* and *c*, and under *d*. Next lead strand *g* over *f* and *e* then under *a* from the opposite side, and so on. Rule: Across the front from first one side and then the other, and over two and under one toward the opposite side.

Fig. 160: The *Nine-Strand French Sennit* is begun with the strands divided 5-4. Lead strand *i* across the front, then over *h* and *g*, and under *f* and *e* toward the opposite side. Next lead strand *a* over *b* and *c*, then under *d* and *i* toward the opposite side. Rule: Use the odd strand on either side, then across the front, over two and under two toward the opposite side.

Fig. 161: The *Five-Strand Running Sennit* is begun by leading the outside strand on either side down across the front, and over two instead of one as in the three-strand method. Repeat alternately from each opposite side, bringing strand *e* down across and over *d* and *c*. Next bring strand *a* down across and over *b* and *e*, repeating this procedure as many times as necessary for the desired length of braid.

Fig. 162: The *Five-Strand Crabber's Eye Sennit* is begun with the strands divided 3-2. Strand *e* is led down under from right to left; then it is passed between *b* and *c* and over *c* toward the right, or back to its own side. Next strand *a* is led down under from left to right and between *d* and *e* and over *e* toward the left, or its own side. Remember at this point to visualize strand *e* in the position it should be in after the last move and not as it is shown in the illustration. This is very important to prevent confusion while braiding sennits that are constructed by leading the strands around and in back, then toward their own side again, as the descriptive text keeps pace with the imaginary braid and will not correspond with the illustration of the strands as they are lettered after the first moves. Continue by leading strand *d* down under from right to left, then under two and over one toward the right side, or in other words between *c* and *a* and over *a*. Proceed by leading *b* down from left to right and between *e* and *d* and over *d*. The key to this braid is down under from left to right, then right to left, going under one and over one from one side, then under two and over one from the other side.

Fig. 163: The *Six-Strand Round Sennit* is begun with the strands divided 3-3. Start by leading strand *a* down and around in back from left to right, then over *f* and under *e* and over *d* to the inside of *c*. Next lead strand *f* down and around in back from right to left, then over *b*, under *c* and over *a* to the inside of *d*. Rule: Down and around in back, then over one, under one and over one toward its own side. The strands should be carefully held in place for this braid; otherwise the key will be lost and it will have to be started over again.

Fig. 164: The *Six-Strand Half Round Sennit* is begun with its strands divided 3-3. Start with strand *a* down and under from left to right and up between *d* and *e*, over *d*, then across to the left side or group. Next lead strand *f* down and under from right to left and up between *c* and *a* and over *a* to the right side or group. Continue by bringing strand *b* down and over left to right and up between *f* and *d*, and over *f* to the left side, and so on. The rule is down and under from first one side and then the other, then under two and over one and back to its own side.

Fig. 165: The *Eight-Strand Square Sennit* is begun with its strands divided 4-4. Start by leading strand *h* down under and around from right to left, then up between *b* and *c* and over *c* and *d* which will place it on the inside of *e*. Next lead strand *a* down under and around from left to right and up between *e* and *f*, then over *e* and *h* to the inside of *d*. Continue by repeating the same process with strand *g* and so on. Rule: Each strand goes down under and around, then under two and over two and back to its own side.

Plate 18—END ROPE KNOTS

Fig. 166 A: The *Three-Strand Crown Knot* is used to start the preparation of a back splice or as a basis for various other knots. Strand *c* is brought down over *a*, then *b* is brought over *c* and passed through the bight of *a*, as indicated by the drawn line. This completes the operation.

B: This shows how the knot appears after each strand has been crowned as explained in 166 A.

Fig. 167 A: The *Three-Strand Wall Knot* is the opposite of a crown knot. In other words you wall up and crown down. Each strand of a wall knot comes up through the bight of the strand next to it, whereas each strand of a crown knot goes down through the bight of the next strand. Strand *b* goes over *a* and then through the bight of *c*. Strand *c* is likewise passed over *b*, and through the bight of *a* as indicated by the drawn line.

B: This illustration shows the knot as it appears after the operation is complete and the strands have been drawn taut. This knot is used back-to-back for a shroud knot, in joining two ropes. There are also various other uses for it, such as finishing off seizings or forming a basis for other knots. This knot, and all other end rope knots, can be tied with any number of strands by using a repetition of the same key.

Fig. 168 A: The *Three-Strand Lanyard Knot* is tied by making a wall knot first, then passing each strand up through the bight of the following strand and pulling

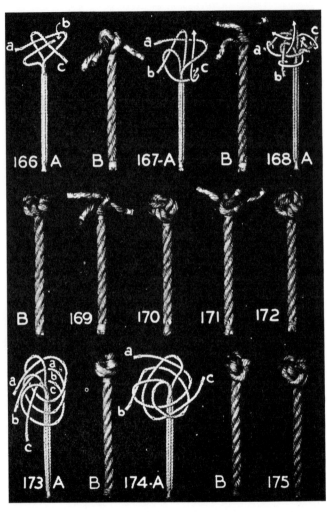

Plate 18—END ROPE KNOTS

taut after the last pass has been completed. Strand *a* is passed through the bight of *c*, then *b* goes through the bight of *a*, and *c* is likewise tucked through the bight of *b*, as illustrated by the drawn lines.

B: This shows the same knot pulled taut. This is an ideal knot to use as a base for building up other knots, as it pulls up in a neat, uniform manner and holds fast.

Fig. 169: The *Three-Strand Single Manrope Knot* has a wall knot as a base, and a crown knot is then tied on top of the wall knot. This provides the framework for a double version of the same knot. In years gone by it was used to form the cat-o'-ninetails.

Fig. 170: The *Three-Strand Double Manrope Knot* follows the same method of construction as the single version of this knot, except that the strands are doubled. After the single pass is completed, the knot is doubled by following each pass around on the wall part and then repeating the same procedure on the crown part, until the knot is completely doubled. To finish off, work the slack out by pulling the strands up taut. This knot is used on the end of gangway lines and for various other purposes.

Fig. 171: The *Three-Strand Single Stopper Knot* includes a crown knot which is formed to start the operation. This is followed by a wall knot around the base. The knot is then pulled tight. However, if it is going to be doubled, enough slack should be left to allow for the additional tucks.

Fig. 172: The *Three-Strand Double Stopper Knot* can likewise be doubled from the single version of this knot by following the same procedure used for the manrope knot. However the crown part is doubled first instead of the wall part as in the previous method. Continue by doubling the wall part as already explained, and then pull the strands up snugly into place. This knot can be used as a stopper on the end of a line or as a shroud knot, when two of the knots are formed back to back. Almost all other types of end rope knots can be used similarly.

Fig. 173 A: The *Matthew Walker Knot* at first looks rather difficult to tie but is really simple when the illustrations are closely followed. Begin by taking the first strand lying nearest the right, which is here designated as strand *a*. Pass it around the body or standing part of the rope and up under its own part, forming an overhand knot. Then take the next strand, which is designated as strand *b*, and repeat the same move. The last strand which is strand *c* is then tucked in the same manner. Care should be used in pulling the strands of this knot taut, as each strand should lay around the knot in a uniform manner and in its proper place.

B: When completed the knot will appear as it does here after being worked up and pulled taut. This knot is used on the end of rigging lanyards. It will not slip.

Fig. 174 A: The *Three-Strand Single Diamond Knot* can be tied by using a number of different keys. The key used in this illustration shows the strands laid out in the form of a flat weave similar to the Turk's head construction. It will be noted that strand *a* is passed around over *c* and *b*, then under *b* and over *c* again and under the bight of *b*, then under *c*. Strand *b* is passed over *a* and *c*, then under *c* and over *a*, then under the bight of *c* and passed out underneath *a*. Strand *c* is passed over *b* and *a*, then under *a* and over *b* again and under the bight of *a*, then out through *b*.

B: This shows the knot after it is pulled up taut and the weave is finished. The two-strand version of the knot is used to unite the chin straps of cavalry hats and is sometimes used by boy scouts for the same purpose.

Fig. 175: The *Three-Strand Double Diamond Knot* follows the same key as illustrated in Plate 19, Fig. 176 B, for doubling the strands with additional passes. It will be noted that by continuing each parallel strand around as they are illustrated with the first tuck in this key, the weave will produce a double diamond knot, whereas if the weave is split as in Fig. 176 C, a sennit knot will be formed.

Plate 19—END ROPE KNOTS AND SPLICES

Fig. 176 A: The *Three-Strand Sennit Knot* is begun by first tying a diamond knot which has a key, illustrated here, that is different from the preceding method shown in Plate 18, Fig. 174. Strand *a* is passed around and tucked through the bight of *b*. Strand *b* is likewise passed around and tucked through the bight of *c*. Strand *c* is now brought around as illustrated and passed through the bight of *a*.

B: This shows the next step of the operation with strands *a, b* and *c* passed down and parallel to the next or following part of the knot that leads down through the weave. This move is necessary in order to convert the diamond knot into a sennit knot. The bights have been purposely pulled out to further clarify the operation.

C: The weave of the knot is continued here with the illustration of the next or last tuck to finish the operation. After the working ends of the strands have received their last tuck, they will now lead out from underneath the knot and point down. The four-strand weave is next split in the middle and each working strand is now passed over the two following bottom cross strands, then through the center of the weave and out under the two top cross strands. This operation will complete the sennit weave. The bights have also been left pulled out here to help clarify the explanation.

D: This shows the knot as it appears after the slack

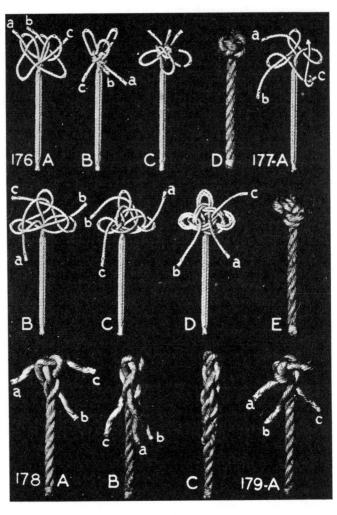

Plate 19—END ROPE KNOTS AND SPLICES

60

has been taken out of the bights and the weave has been drawn up neat and snug. White line has been used for the preliminary steps as in most of the other end rope designs in order to make the operation as clear as possible. This knot is used in a variety of combinations to form many beautiful rose knot designs.

Fig. 177 A: The *Three-Strand Star Knot* is a rather difficult knot to explain, but each move in the key illustrated here is simplicity itself. Numerous complicated ways of tying the star knot have been called to the author's attention in bygone years. However this method, originated by the author in the China Sea, far surpasses any of the other methods of tying this knot. It is a simple, uniform manner of operation that the novice will have no trouble in duplicating if he studies closely the structural design of the knot. It will be noted that the knot is begun by laying out an underhand eye with each strand, then the end of the line of the next or adjoining strand is passed through the eyes in the manner illustrated.

B: The next step in the formation of the knot is shown here, the working ends being designated as *a,* *b* and *c*. They have each been passed over the top of the knot and out through each following eye.

C: The parts underneath are now doubled by passing the working ends around and up through the eyes. The working ends of the strands are rotating around the body of the knot as they are passed from right to left, and care should be taken to observe the structural formation of the pattern that is assuming shape at this point. The top parts of the knot are now doubled like the bottom parts, completing the next step in the operation. There is only one more series of passes to make from this point in order to finish the knot.

D: The last move is shown here, the working ends

being brought back parallel around each eye in the opposite direction from the general trend of the weave. This pass will double the eyes. The ends now come out through the center of the knot as shown. This series of illustrations has purposely been laid out flat to help clarify the construction, but of course in actual practice the knot is formed on top of the rope and not on the side, as shown here.

E: The completed *Star Knot* as it appears after being worked up and pulled taut, with the ends cut off short on top of the knot. As a rule a lanyard knot is used as a base on which to form this type of knot, although these illustrations omit the lanyard knot in order to make the construction appear less complicated. This is one of the most popular of all the decorative knots that were tied by the old time shellbacks. It makes a very beautiful design when tied with six parts instead of three, as shown here. The same key is used in the making of this knot regardless of the number of strands.

Fig. 178 A: The *Three-Strand Back Splice* is begun with a crown knot. Then each strand is tucked over the next strand and under the second strand. In this illustration strands *a* and *c* have not yet been tucked, while strand *b* has received one tuck. The splicing is continued by tucking strands *a* and *c* in the prescribed manner.

B: This shows the splice after strands *a, b* and *c* have each been tucked once, or in other words, one round of tucks has been completed. Make several tucks, and taper the splice down by splitting each strand in half for each remaining tuck. Then pull taut and trim all strands.

C: This shows the splice as it will appear when finished. This splice may be tapered or left untapered. However, three or four rounds of tucks should be made if the strands are going to be cut off without being tapered.

Fig. 179 A: The *Three-Strand Sailmaker's Back Splice* begins with a crown knot as in the regular splice. But instead of going over one and under one, each tuck is made over, around, and then under the next, or following strand, which brings them out with the lay of the rope. Strands *a*, *b* and *c* have each received one tuck in this illustration. The bight of strand *b* has been left pulled out in order to give a clearer picture of the way the strands are tucked. This splice is worked down and finished off in the same manner as in the preceding method. Sailmakers use this neat form of splicing for awnings. Illustration 179 B, showing the completed splice, will be found on Plate 20.

Plate 20—EYE AND CUT SPLICES

Fig. 179 B: This shows the finished splice that was explained in Plate 19, Fig. 179 A.

Figs. 180 A, B and C: The *Three-Strand Eye Splice* is made as follows: Unlay the rope a sufficient distance, and make an eye of the required size; tuck the bottom strand under one strand against the lay and place the middle strand under the next strand in the same manner. Turn the splice over and tuck the remaining strand as previously described in Fig. 178. Strands *a* and *b* are shown tucked in Fig. 180 A. Fig. 180 B shows the splice turned over, with strand *c* tucked. Tuck each strand against the lay a second time, over one and under one, and repeat as many times as desired. After tapering down to finish off, the splice will appear as in Fig. 180 C. This splice and all other splices can be rolled under the foot or hammered down to insure a neat, close-fitting job.

Fig. 181: The *Three-Strand Sailmaker's Eye Splice* is begun by unlaying the rope and making the first tucks as

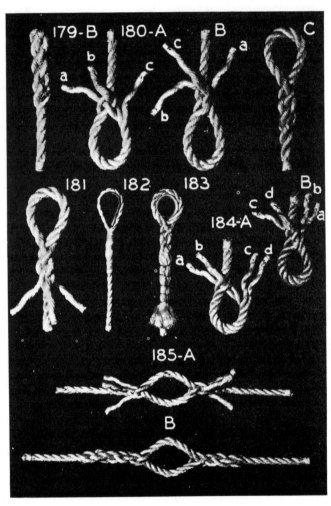

Plate 20—EYE AND CUT SPLICES

though for the regular eye splice. Then continue by making the sailmaker's tucks (See Fig. 179 A), until the required number has been made. The splice is tapered down and the strands are cut off short to finish. This shows the splice after the first set of sailmaker's tucks has been completed.

Fig. 182: In the *Eye Splice Served,* the eye is bent around a thimble, then spliced in, tapered down and served in the usual manner. A thimble is used to prevent a hook from chafing the rope.

Fig. 183: The *Round Thimble Eye Splice with Ends Frayed* is a round thimble spliced into an eye with the ends frayed out and hitched along the body of the rope with marline.

Figs. 184 A and B: The *Four-Strand Eye Splice* is a repetition of the three-strand method, except at the beginning. The bottom strand is tucked under two strands, and the other strands are tucked under one each. Strand *a* in Fig. 184 A is shown tucked under two strands as described, and strand *b* under one strand. Turn the splice over and tuck strands *c* and *d* accordingly. The splice will then appear as in Fig. 184 B. Continue by tucking over one and under one against the lay, until the required number of tucks has been made.

Fig. 185 A: The *Cut Splice* is made by measuring off the required distance, depending on the size of the eye desired. Then splice each end into the standing part of the other rope. This illustration shows the first set of tucks with the end of each adjoining rope.

B: Shows the completed splice. The splice is used to form an eye or collar in the bight of a rope.

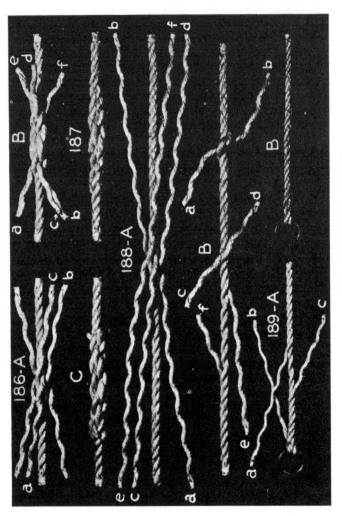

Plate 21—SHORT AND LONG SPLICES

Plate 21—SHORT AND LONG SPLICES

Fig. 186 A: The *Three-Strand Short Splice* is the strongest and most secure method of uniting two ropes. It is stronger than the long splice, but increases the diameter of the rope, so that the spliced portion of the rope may be unable to pass over the sheave of a block. To begin this splice, unlay the ends of each rope, and marry the strands as shown in the illustration. In marrying a rope, one strand of one rope comes between two strands of the other, as shown by strand *a*, which comes between the two strands *b* and *c*. The work will be found much simpler to execute if a temporary seizing is placed at the point where both ropes have been married. This will serve to hold the ropes in position until the first tucks are made. The strands on the right-hand side are, for the moment, left alone. Begin with any strand on the left. Tuck it over one and under one against the lay.

B: After strands *a*, *b*, and *c* have been tucked, strands *d, e* and *f* are tucked once each. The splice is begun on both sides, there now being one round of tucks. Two more tucks are put in with each strand, making three rounds of tucks in all, which is the proper amount for a secure splice.

C: This shows the *Short Splice* after two rounds of tucks have been made. After another round of tucks has been finished, the splice is then rolled under the foot and pounded with a fid or mallet, to make it round and work the strands into place. The strands are then cut off, but not too close, or they may work out when tension is applied. The splice can be tapered by following directions in Plate 19, Fig. 178 A.

Fig. 187: The *Three-Strand Sailmaker's Short Splice* is begun by marrying the strands of each rope. Choose any

67

two strands lying next to each other, in order to have one adjacent strand from each rope. Then, instead of going over one and under one as in the common splice, tuck them around one another. As there is a right and wrong way of tucking these strands in the sailmaker's splices, the following method should be followed to eliminate the possibility of making any errors: When the strands have been married, each set of adjoining strands is tied together by forming an overhand knot with the lay of the rope, or in the same manner as for finishing off a long splice. The splice is now continued by tucking each strand over, around, and then under the next, or following strand in the standing part of the rope, which brings them out with the lay of the rope after each tuck. This method is repeated until three rounds of tucks have been made. (The example shown in the illustration has been tapered down after only one round of tucks in order to fit into the limited space.)

Fig. 188 A: The *Three-Strand Long Splice* (over and under style), though weaker than the short splice and requiring more rope, does not increase the diameter of the rope appreciably and therefore can be run over a sheave or pulley without jamming in the block. To begin, unlay the strands of both ropes four or five times farther than in a short splice. (In reality, the strands are unlaid much farther than shown in the illustration, since it was necessary to make the splice shorter in order to get the work into the photograph.) Then marry the strands as shown here, and group them off into pairs. The next step is to take strand *a* and unlay it a short distance. Then take its mate, strand *b* and lay it into the groove that was made when strand *a* was removed. When strand *b* has been laid up to strand *a*, and they meet, tie an overhand knot with both strands to hold them temporarily. Next, go back to the center and knot strands *c* and *d* together, so they will remain where they are. Take strand *f* and unlay it to the left the same distance that strand *a* was unlaid to the right. Then lay strand *e* into the groove left when strand *f* was taken out.

B: This shows how the splice looks after the preceding steps have been taken. (The overhand knots have been tied with only one set of strands in this illustration.) Join strands *a* and *b* together on the right, with an overhand knot; and strands *c* and *d* are together in the center. Strand *f* has been unlaid, and strand *e* is being laid into the groove until it reaches strand *f*. The next and final step is the disposal of the ends of each set of strands after they have been joined together with an overhand knot, tied with the lay of the rope as illustrated by strands *a* and *b*. This is done by splicing each one of the separate ends over and under against the lay of the rope with a sufficient number of tucks which can be tapered at the end. The procedure of finishing off a splice of this type can be accomplished in several ways, but the method explained here is probably the most commonly used. The four-strand long splice is prepared in the same manner as the three-strand method, except that the operation requires an additional allowance for the extra strands after the two ropes have been married. In other words each set of strands must be laid up and joined together an equal distance apart. They are then finished in the regular manner.

Figs. 189 A and B: The *Chain Splice* is tied as follows: Unlay the rope a considerable distance and reeve strands *b* and *c* through the end link of the chain; then unlay strand *a* quite some distance down the rope; tuck strand *b* under strand *c*, and lay up strand *c* in the groove vacated by strand *a*. Join them together with an overhand knot, disposing of the strands by tucking against the lay, as in a regular long splice, with strand *b* also tucked over and under against the lay to finish. Fig. 189 A illustrates the open splice at the beginning; and Fig. 189 B shows how it looks when complete.

Plate 22—SPLICES, GROMMETS AND WHIPPINGS

Figs. 190 A and B: The *Horseshoe Splice* is begun by unlaying a short piece of rope as shown in Fig. 190 A and splicing it into the standing parts of another piece of rope which has been bent in horseshoe fashion. The completed splice will then appear as in Fig. 190 B. This splice was formerly used to separate the legs of a pair of shrouds.

Fig. 191: The *Adjustable Halter* is begun by measuring off the proper length of rope according to the table below. Form an eye with the part of rope used for the long bight or nose-piece. Tuck it under one strand of the other part of rope representing the head-piece. Tuck the head-piece under two strands of the nose-piece, toward the right, to complete the eye. Bring the nose-piece around to form the proper length of bight and splice it into the head-piece. Adjust the halter to the animal and secure the lead to the loop if it is desired.

TABLE FOR ADJUSTABLE HALTER

	Diameter of rope *in inches*	Total length of rope *in feet*	Length left for lead *in feet*
Large cattle	½	12	6
Medium cattle	⅜	11½	6
Small cattle	⅜	11	6
Calves and sheep	¼	7½	4

Fig. 192 A: The *Three-Strand Grommet* represents a type of rope work that can be utilized for making many different articles, such as strops, chest handles, and quoits. It is made from a single strand of rope, as follows: First, take a piece of rope of the desired thickness; determine the circumference of the grommet you wish to make, then measure off three and one-half times this circumference. (In other words, if the circumference is one foot, three and one-half feet is the proper measurement.) Next, cut the rope and unlay one strand. Tie an overhand knot in this strand with the lay of the rope as shown in the illustration. (The strands have purposely been left short, in order to fit them into the photograph.)

B: Begin by laying up one strand, or if desired the ends of both sides of the overhand knot can be laid up at the same time, which will produce the same result. When the ends meet there will be a grommet of two strands as shown here.

C: Continue the strand around again, making a three-strand grommet as illustrated here. When the strands meet again at the finish, halve them and tie an overhand knot, then proceed to dispose of the ends as in the common long splice. In this case strands *a* and *b* represent the inactive half of the strands which will be tucked into the grommet, while strands *c* and *d* are the parts with which the overhand knot is formed. They are also tucked into the grommet to finish off.

Fig. 193: This illustration shows a *Hemp-Laid Long-Spliced Grommet*. A single strand of tarred hemp is laid up into three strands. When the strand is laid up two turns, cross the strand from the left under or inside the strand from the right, then continue around until the strands meet again and tie an overhand knot. Next, unlay the strands at the overhand knot by a half turn, to make

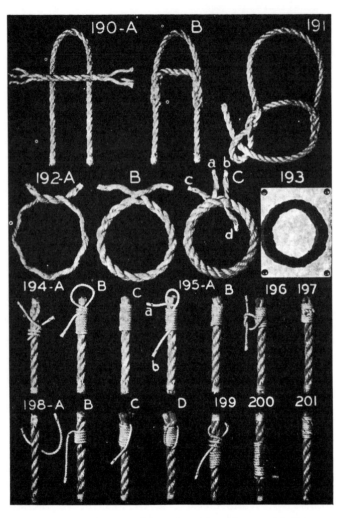

Plate 22—SPLICES, GROMMETS AND WHIPPINGS

them flat, then continue by tucking the ends with a tapered sailmaker's splice.

Fig. 194 A: A *Plain Whipping*. (Whippings are always made with the twine wound against the lay of the rope. It is also customary to work the turns toward the end of the rope.) Fig. 194 A shows the beginning of the whipping. One end of the twine is placed near the end of the rope, and then run back a short distance before the turns are begun.

B: After the desired number of turns has been wound around the rope, the end of the twine is laid in the direction shown in this illustration. Then three or four more turns are wound around the end of the rope with the bight of the twine.

C: After the finishing turns have been wound around, as just described, the last turn is drawn tight, and both ends are cut off close to finish the whipping.

Fig. 195 A: The *Temporary Whipping* is made by first laying a bight on the rope a short distance from the end. A number of turns are taken about the rope and on top of the bight. End *a* of the whipping twine is put through the loop, and end *b*, which forms the bight, is drawn until the loop is under the turns. Both ends of the twine are then cut off close.

B: This figure shows the whipping after the ends have been cut off short to finish the whipping.

Fig. 196: The *American Whipping*, called by this name in England, is a variation of the plain whipping. Both ends of the twine are brought up in the middle of the turns and joined with a reef knot. The reef knot should be made in the groove between two strands of the rope, so that it can be pushed down between them, beneath the turns. In this case the bottom part of the reef knot has been pulled down under the turns, but the top part of the knot has not yet been pulled up taut.

Fig. 197: The *Ordinary Whipping* is similar to the American whipping except that instead of joining the ends of the twine with a reef knot that is pulled up underneath the turns, the reef knot in this method is left tightly knotted on top of the turns. The ends are then cut off close to the knot to finish the operation.

Fig. 198 A: The *Palm and Needle Whipping* at first appears to be rather difficult, but it is actually one of the simplest types of whippings. First, take a suitable length of twine, then thread it in a sail needle and wax it well. Proceed by stitching it through the rope as shown here.

B: Next, take the proper number of turns around the rope and the short end of the twine, keeping each turn as taut as possible.

C: When enough turns have been taken, the twine is stitched through the rope again. Then bring the twine down on top of the turns, giving it the proper position along the lay of the rope. It is next stitched under another strand and brought back up again over the top of the turns. This operation is repeated three times, until all the grooves between the rope strands have strands of the twine resting in them.

D: Finally, an additional stitch is taken through the rope with the twine, which is then cut off. The whipping, if properly made, will look like this illustration.

Note: Very few people know the proper length to make a whipping. Some keep winding turns around the rope until it "looks right." But this is not a dependable method. A whipping should be as long as the diameter of the rope upon which it is placed. In the illustrations, large white line has been used purposely, and an exceptional number of turns has also been taken in order to clarify the pictures. However, sail twine is the most commonly used material for work of this sort.

Fig. 199: The *Plain Whipping in the Middle of a Line*

74

serves a special purpose. In most cases, a whipping is used to prevent the end of a rope from fraying out or becoming unlaid. But it sometimes becomes necessary to place a whipping in the center of a rope or other object. In order to do this, leave several turns slack, and pass the end of the whipping twine under them, as shown. Each turn is then hove taut, and the end pulled to take out the slack.

Fig. 200: The *Seaman's Whipping* is made in the following way: First take a piece of waxed sail twine of the required length, then lay one end of this along the rope's end to be whipped and, while holding it in place under the thumb, wind the twine tightly around it and the rope. These turns are continued until near the end of the rope; then lay another piece of twine in the form of a bight along the rope's end and take about four more whipping turns over this twine. The end of the line is then passed through the eye of its bight. The bight is pulled from under the turns, at the same time heaving the end of the twine up snug and tight under the whipping turns. This is an excellent method for securing the end of the line under the turns, as it leaves no excess slack to work out at the finish. The illustration shows the end of the whipping line passed through the eye of the bight, prior to its being pulled through under the turns.

Fig. 201: The *French* or *Grapevine Whipping* is a very secure and unique method of whipping the end of a rope. A suitable length of whipping twine is taken, and an overhand knot is tied a short distance back from the end of the rope. Next, a continuous row of half hitches is put on against the lay of the rope, until the end is almost reached. Then two loose hitches are taken, and the end of the twine is placed under them; the hitches are drawn taut and the slack end pulled to complete the whipping.

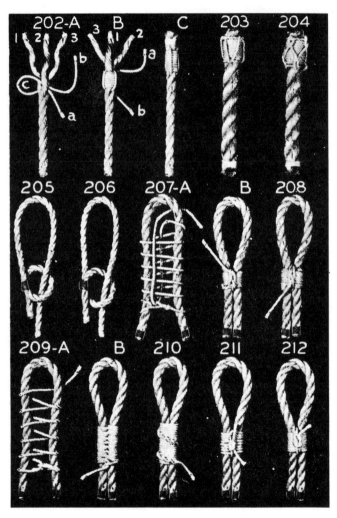

Plate 23—WHIPPINGS AND SEIZINGS

Plate 23—WHIPPINGS AND SEIZINGS

Fig. 202 A: The *Sailmaker's Whipping* is made as follows: The end of the rope is opened for a short distance; a bight of the twine is put around one strand, leading the ends between the other two strands, as shown in the illustration. End *a* in this case is the moving end, and end *b* is the standing end. The strands are next laid up again, and the proper number of turns taken around the rope. Then bight *c* is brought up and passed over the end of strand 1.

B: This illustration shows the whipping after bight *c* has been passed over strand 1. It is next heaved tight by the standing end of the twine, and the standing end is carried up alongside strand 3. Then the working and standing ends are knotted tightly together between the strands and trimmed off.

C: This shows the whipping after it is finished. The end of the rope has been seized on top of the whipping for clearness, but ordinarily the strands are trimmed close to the top part of the work.

Fig. 203: *Snaking* is an old method of securing a whipping or seizing on a heavy rope or cable. When as many turns have been placed on the rope as desired, put the sail needle through the rope and haul the twine tight. The working end is then taken over and under the upper and lower turns of the whipping as shown.

Fig. 204: The *Herringbone Whipping* is somewhat similar to the whipping just described, except that when the twine is put through the upper and lower turns of the whipping, they are half-hitched rather than merely stitched through.

Fig. 205: The *Outside Clinch Seizing* is a running knot formed by reeving the standing part of the rope through the eye of a simple clinch seizing.

Fig. 206: The *Inside Clinch* is similar in method to the preceding, except that it is somewhat more secure. When hauled taut around a spar or other object, it jams on itself. While it is somewhat more difficult to release than the outside clinch, it is a good knot to use when a turn is to be taken about an object and after being drawn taut must be slipped rather quickly. These clinches, Figs. 205 and 206, have a single cross seizing.

Figs. 207 A and B: The *Flat Seizing* is used only as a light seizing, when the strain is not too great and there is equal tension on the two parts or ropes to be seized together. First, take a sufficient length of marline or seizing twine and splice an eye in one end. Then place it around both of the ropes or shrouds and pass the unspliced end through its own eye, heaving it taut. Take the required number of turns, passing the end of the seizing line beneath the turns and between the two parts being seized together, then out through the eye of the seizing line, as shown in Fig. 207 A. Next, take a round turn with the seizing line, passing it between the lines and over the turns already made, and heaving it taut. Then pass the seizing line around again, making two turns before finishing off with a braided clove hitch, as illustrated in Fig. 207 B. These additional turns are called "frapping turns."

Fig. 208: The *Round Seizing* is stronger than the flat seizing, and is to be preferred where the strain is very pronounced. Begin as in the flat version, but make an odd number of passes (say, seven or nine) before reeving the end of the seizing line beneath the turns and back through its own eye; then heave taut. These turns make up the first layer and are called the "lower turns." Next, the top or upper turns are made with an even number of passes (one less than the lower turns) which places the upper turns in the grooves formed between the lower ones. The end of the seizing line is then tucked under the last of the lower turns and hove taut.

Figs. 209 A and B: The *Racking* or *Nippered Seizing* is the best method to use when an unequal strain is placed on two shrouds, as when turning in a deadeye. The seizing line should be well stretched before being used in a seizing of this type. Begin as in the flat or round seizing, by forming a turn around the two parts to be seized, then reeving the end of the seizing line through its own eye. The turns are started in a sort of figure-of-eight fashion, as illustrated. After making about ten passes (if the strain is to be severe), start the second passes back in the direction of the beginning, fitting them in between the grooves left by the first turns. Finish off by reeving the end of the seizing line through its own eye again. Then tie an overhand knot and cut off short. A slightly different method of making this seizing can be used if desired. Before starting the second turns or passes, form a half hitch on the inside of the last figure-of-eight loop, and then follow back toward the beginning, as already described. The cross or frapping turns may also be applied to finish off.

Fig. 210: The *French* or *Grapevine Seizing* is an ornamental type of seizing, made by half-hitching one strand around the body of the seized parts. It is started by overlapping one strand with the working part, and can be finished either by tying an overhand knot up close or by tucking the end under.

Fig. 211: The *Necklace Seizing* is begun in the same way as the racking seizing, by taking the required number of figure-of-eight turns, then tucking the end of the seizing line under the last turn and across the front to form a reef knot with the line from the other side.

Fig. 212: The *Middle Seizing* closely follows the temporary whipping, Plate 22, Fig. 195, except that the bottom strand forming the loop is cut off short. Then the other end of the seizing line, after being rove through the eye of the loop on the opposite side, is passed around the seizing two times to form the cross or frapping turns. The seizing is finished off with a reef knot, as illustrated.

Plate 24—GENERAL KNOTS AND TIES

Fig. 213: The *Sheet Bend with Toggle* is tied by placing the toggle between the lines, as shown. This method prevents the knot from jamming and also gives it added resistance under tension.

Fig. 214: The *Toggle Bend* is a very useful knot to use when the bights of two ropes are to be bent together. It is easily formed and can be cast off instantly in an emergency. Slip the eye of one line over the eye of the other. Then take both parts of one bight, draw them up through the opening and insert the toggle.

Fig. 215: The *Sheepshank with Toggle* is a method of tying the sheepshank so its ends are more secure when tension is uneven—especially if the ends of the rope are inaccessible.

Fig. 216: The *Florist's Knot* can be easily followed from the illustration. It is used by florists for securing twine.

Fig. 217: The *Binder Twine Bend* is made by first forming a bight in one rope or twine. Then bring the end of the other piece up through the bight, take a turn around the bight, and pass the end out through its own loop in the same direction as the end of the other part. Now pull the knot up taut. This knot is used for tying together the ends of balls of binder twine used on grain harvesters.

Fig. 218: The *Grocer's Hitch* is used around the top

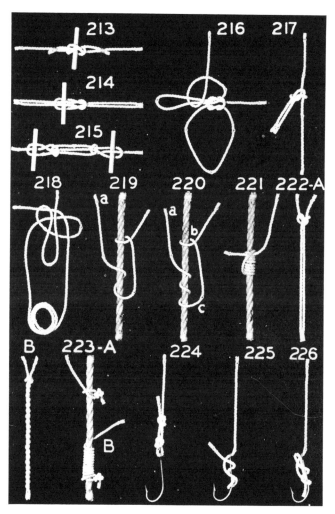

Plate 24—GENERAL KNOTS AND TIES

81

of paper sacks, etc. The round turns at the bottom indicate how twine is passed around the neck of sacks in order to secure them.

Fig. 219: A *Tent Stake Hitch* such as that shown here can be used when rope and stakes are dry. To tighten, pressure is applied by heaving on line *a*.

Fig. 220: The *Tent Stake* or *Storm Hitch* is used by circus men to make ropes fast. To make the line tight, push down at *b;* to slacken, push up at *c*. Two men work together, one of them heaving on line *a*.

Fig. 221: The *Fire Hose Hitch* is used extensively for hauling water hose to the upper floors or roof of a building. The knot is usually placed just below one of the couplings connecting the lengths of hose together. The hitch is made as follows: Take several turns about the hose, bring the end back over the turns and form a half hitch. The end shown on top in the illustration is the hauling end, while the lower end may be used to secure the hose in any position on the building, or to a ladder.

Fig. 222 A: The *Electrician's* or *Underwriter's Knot* is used by electricians for securing wires in electrical fixtures. It is actually a left-handed wall knot as shown in the accompanying illustration.

B: This shows the knot as it appears after being drawn taut on the end of an electric wire.

Fig. 223 A: The *Fireman's Hitch* illustrates the method used by firemen for various kinds of tying purposes. It can be used for hoisting hose. The top illustration shows how the hitch is started to begin the operation.

B: This is how the completed tie appears after a dozen round turns have been taken for added security.

Fig. 224: The *Fisherman's Knot Tie* is a simple method of securing a line to a hook, or for joining the ends of two leaders together.

Fig. 225: The *Fishhook Tie* shown here represents another of the many different methods that are used for attaching fishhooks to a line. Its form of construction is clearly illustrated and needs no explanation.

Fig. 226: The *Fishhook Tie* shown here is somewhat different from the preceding method, but close study of its form of construction will show "plainer than words can describe" how it is tied.

Plate 25—MISCELLANEOUS KNOTS

Fig. 227: The *Carpenter's Hitch* is used by carpenters to fasten chalk lines to nails or hooks.

Fig. 228: The *Marten Knot* is used as a temporary tie to prevent the unlaid strands on the end of a rope from fraying. It is tied by forming an overhand knot with an outside strand around the standing part of the rope in the manner shown.

Fig. 229: The *Buntline Hitch* or *Studding-Sail Tack Bend* is made by taking an inside clove hitch around the standing part. This hitch will jam hard and does not slacken. It is used to make fast the tack of the studding sail.

Fig. 230: The *Buntline Hitch with Round Turn* is the same as the preceding except for a round turn taken for added security.

Fig. 231: The *Lobster Buoy Hitch* is quite simple to construct and needs no explanation.

Fig. 232: The *Bag Knot* is one of the numerous ways millers have for securing tops of bags.

Fig. 233: The *Miller's Knot* shown here is probably the most widely used of all millers' ties. However, many millers prefer other variations, such as a slippery clove hitch or a round turn with a reef knot to secure the ends.

Fig. 234: The *Sack Knot* is still another method of forming the various types of millers' ties.

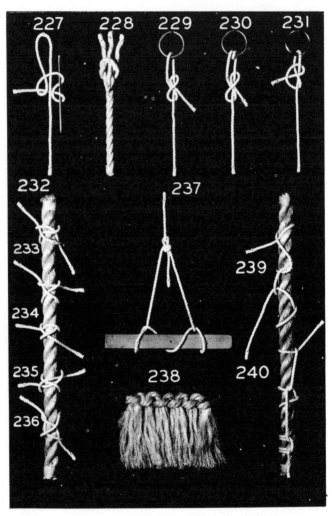

Plate 25—MISCELLANEOUS KNOTS

Fig. 235: The *Sack Knot*, second method, is a variation of this form of tie. Study of the illustration will make plain how it differs from the preceding method.

Fig. 236: The *Blood Knot* is another simple method used in tying sacks. Like the preceding sack knots, it is so simple that the method of tying it needs no explanation.

Fig. 237: The *Edge Plank Sling* or *Scaffold Hitch* is often used by riggers for various purposes, such as to sling a plank on its side. In order to do this, first take several turns around the plank, the number depending upon the length of the object to be slung. When the turns are near the end on each side, make a hitch as illustrated, and join the two lines with a bowline to keep the planking balanced steadily, so that the ends do not tip.

Fig. 238: The *Railway Sennit*, is begun by unlaying two strands from a rope and twisting them together. The remaining strand is cut into three-inch lengths. Then each piece is middled and passed through the rope between the two strands, one end on each side of the point where the strands cross. Continue until the desired length has been attained. This type of sennit is used as chafing gear, being wrapped around stays and lifts and lazy jacks to protect sails in sailing ships. It can also be used on the booms of steam vessels to prevent the wire cargo-runners from striking the underside of the boom and chipping off the paint.

Fig. 239: The *Hoisting Hitch* is used by riggers for various lifting purposes. Its form of construction can be followed easily.

Fig. 240: The *Hoisting Hitch*, second method, shown here is tied in a different manner from the preceding illustration. However, its construction should not be difficult to understand if the tie is closely observed.

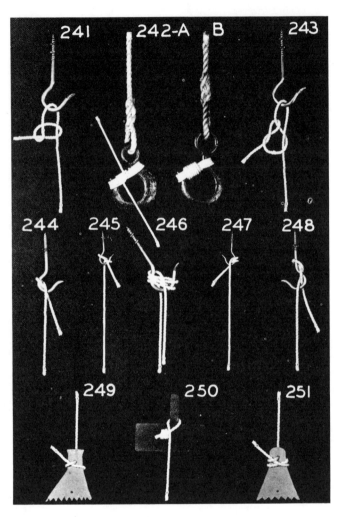

Plate 26—MISCELLANEOUS HITCHES

Plate 26—MISCELLANEOUS HITCHES

Fig. 241: The *Shank Hitch* shown here is used on a hook with small rope.

Fig. 242 A: The method of *Mousing a Hook* is a valuable thing to know when using a hook on which the rope is to remain for some time. There is always a danger that the hook will throw off its load when the line is slack. Therefore a hook should always be moused in order to safeguard against this. There are several ways of doing this, but the most reliable method is as follows: Take several turns around the bill and the back of the hook with a length of marline. When enough turns have been taken, cross the ends in opposite directions, as shown here. Continue by applying tight frapping turns in both directions from the center. After this has been done, add a layer of riding turns back to the center from both ends, then finish off by securing the ends with a reef knot.

B: This shows the mousing completed. The reef knot is underneath.

Fig. 243: The *Shank Hitch*, second method, is used where it is desired to upset the hitch when the strain has been removed from the line.

Fig. 244: The *Single Blackwall Hitch* consists of a half hitch crossed through a hook. This is a quick and easy way to secure a rope to a hook for temporary use.

Fig. 245: The *Bill Hitch* is formed in the same manner as a becket hitch, and a sheet bend. The bill hitch, however, is used to hitch a line to a hook, and the sheet bend is used to bend two ropes together.

Fig. 246: The *Racking Hitch* on a hook follows the same method of construction as other forms of racking ties, but it is applied to a hook.

Fig. 247: The *Double Blackwall* or *Stunner Hitch* is more secure than the single Blackwall hitch.

Fig. 248: The *Double Blackwall Hitch*, second method, is made by placing the bight of the rope across the strop on the block which is omitted here. Cross it behind the hook, and then cross it again in front of the hook as illustrated. It holds much better than the single method.

Fig. 249: The *Butcher's Hitch* is the proper knot for suspending a quarter of beef.

Fig. 250: The *Waldo Hitch* is handy for securing the end of a rope to the limb of a tree in order to lower oneself over the edge of a cliff. The rope can be pulled down afterwards by swinging it over the knot. The end is knotted with a two-fold knot.

Fig. 251: The *Flag Hitch* is a method commonly used to make a halyard fast to a flag. Its form of construction can be easily followed.

Plate 27—MISCELLANEOUS KNOTS AND BRAIDS

Fig. 252: The *Thief* or *Bread Bag Knot* differs from the ordinary reef knot in that the ends come out on opposite sides instead of on the same side. The reef knot will bear a strain without slipping, but when tension is applied to the thief knot, it will keep on slipping until the ends are reached and the two lines separate. The thief knot slips when a strain is put on it because the contiguous parts move in the same direction and so there is no friction to make the knot secure. An interesting old yarn, derived from the days of sailing vessels, is told to account for the name of this knot. It is said that on one vessel the cook always fastened the bread container in the galley with a reef or square knot. In his absence the cabin boy would steal food from the galley and invariably tied the modification known as "thief" instead of the true reef knot. Upon seeing the bread box fastened with an improperly tied knot, the cook always knew who to blame, much to the cabin boy's surprise.

Fig. 253: The *Painter's Hitch* shows how painters make the fall rope fast when they suspend the staging with tackles.

Fig. 254: The *Water Bowline* is the same as the ordinary bowline, except that it has an additional half hitch. This knot is used whenever a rope is likely to become soaked with water. The strain taken by the additional half hitch prevents the bowline from drawing tight and becoming difficult to untie.

Fig. 255 A: The *Chinese Button Knot* has been used for centuries by Chinese tailors who employ it for a variety of purposes, such as the forming of soft buttons for pajamas and underwear. These are more comfortable for clothes of this sort than the harder buttons of other varieties and, at the same time, they are almost indestructible. The knot is shown here in a flat pattern exactly as it is tied by the Chinese. After this stage has been reached, the knot is next capsized or flipped over the two working ends of the line and pulled taut.

B: After being adjusted and pulled up properly it will appear as in this illustration.

Fig. 256: The *Sail Twine Stopper Knot* is used for stopping off the end of the twine by taking a number of turns in the manner indicated, after which the needle is drawn through to finish the work.

Fig. 257: The *Climber's* or *Pruner's Saddle* is used by the Park Department of the City of New York, where it is known as a *Taut Knot*. First make a chain braid, and then join the lines together with a bowline. An overhand knot is then tied below the bowline, and the line is passed up through this knot and joined to the other end of the line with two round turns on the top part of the knot, which is followed by an inside hitch, plus another

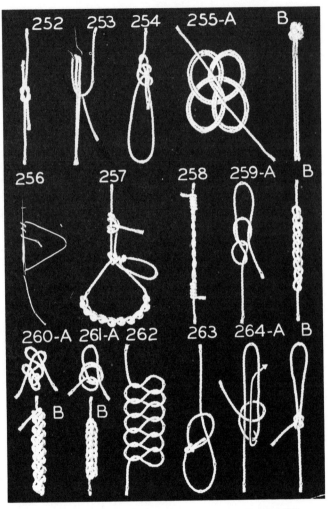

Plate 27—MISCELLANEOUS KNOTS AND BRAIDS

round turn, with the working end of the line leading out from the middle part of the knot as illustrated.

Fig. 258: The *Haywire Bend* is a good way to join the ends of wire together with pliers.

Fig. 259 A: The *Chain Braid* is begun by forming a slip bight in an overhand knot. Then continue the braid by passing each additional bight through the eye of the last bight as illustrated here.

B: This pictures the completed braid. It is used for shortening a line and is often seen on the end of curtain pulls for that reason.

Fig. 260 A: The *Higginbotham Braid* is formed as follows: Tie a slip bight in an overhand knot, then place another bight through the first one from the opposite side as shown here. Continue this procedure, pulling up the eye of each bight as the braid progresses.

B: This pictures the braid as it looks when finished and turned over on the opposite side.

Fig. 261 A: The *Bugler's Braid* is begun by forming two round turns to start with, one laid on top of the other. It is better to fold these round turns or coils to the left as the picture illustrates. Then pass a bight under both round turns (to form another round turn of its own) as shown in the first stage of the operation. Pull the eye of the bight up uniformly as each step of the work progresses and pass each additional bight over the first round turn and under the next two, adjusting the size and shape of the braid with the running part of the line as the work is continued, until the required amount of braid has been reached.

B: This shows the finished braid.

Fig. 262: The *Figure-of-Eight Chain Braid* can be duplicated easily by observing the illustration.

Fig. 263: The *Running Bowline* is simply an ordinary bowline made around the standing part of the line. There is a knack to tying this knot with the free end of the line around the standing part that is made fast. It is better first to form the eye or gooseneck with the working part, which is then led around the standing part, through the gooseneck, around its own part, and back through the gooseneck again to complete the tie. It can be used to slip over the end of a spar or other object in place of the timber hitch.

Fig. 264 A: The *Single Bowline on the Bight* is made by forming a bight and taking a round turn as shown here. Pull the bottom part up through the bight on top, as the drawn line indicates, and at the same time pull the top bight down.

B: The finished bowline is shown here after being pulled taut.

Plate 28—GENERAL KNOT WORK

Fig. 265: *Belaying a Halyard to a Cleat*. This is the correct method of belaying a line to a cleat. The end should not be secured in any manner other than that shown, that is, it should not be further secured by hitches, or other methods. Note that the end of the line can be slipped free quickly and the turns on the cleat cast off.

Fig. 266: The *Plumb Bob Hitch* is used by surveyors for suspending a plumb bob beneath a transit. Its construction is too simple to require an explanation.

Fig. 267: The *False Bowline* is in reality a seized loop, with the gooseneck formed in the manner of a figure-of-eight bowline.

Fig. 268: The *Game Carrier Tie* is a method that is used by hunters for carrying game.

Fig. 269: Shows a way to break twine with the fingers. Jerk the bottom end while holding the top part fast, and

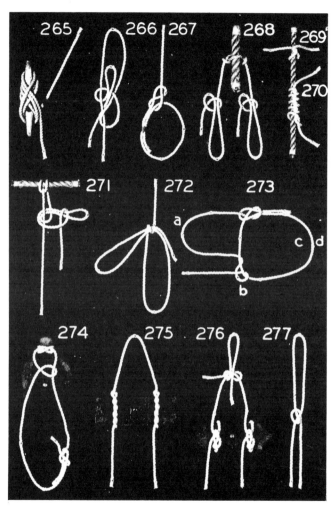

Plate 28—GENERAL KNOT WORK

the twine will break at the cross on top of the fingers.

Fig. 270: The *Hog's Eye* is used to sew sail thread around the edge of an eye in a sail or other canvas of any kind to prevent the cloth from fraying.

Fig. 271: The *Packer's Hitch* is used by packers on packboards and in connection with diamond hitches. The picture clearly illustrates its method of construction.

Fig. 272: The *Bell Ringer's Knot* is designed for a particular purpose. Church bells have a wheel on the axle to which they are hung. The bell rope passes around this wheel, to obtain leverage enough to raise the mouth of the bell upward when it is rung. This operation requires a long rope, most of which lies on the belfry floor when the bell is down. After the bell has been rung, this slack is tied up out of the way with the knot illustrated here. It is nothing more than a hitch on the end of the standing part. The working end of the line is passed back through the hitch to form a slip eye, which will hold securely if the hitch is kept pulled up close to the standing part. A slight pull with the end of the line will release the whole knot instantly. *Tufting* is usually found on the standing part above the hitch for use in grasping the line. It is made by opening the strands and placing short pieces of worsted through them. Then these pieces are trimmed off until they are all the same length.

Fig. 273: The *Hackamore Halter Tie* was used in the early days of the West for breaking wild and unruly horses. Loop *c* goes around the horse's neck, with the lines *d* on top and *b* underneath, *a* goes over the muzzle to complete the arrangement.

Fig. 274: The *Jug Sling* can be used to carry any kind of a jug or bottle. A clove hitch is made around the neck and secured with a half hitch on top. The lines are then adjusted to the required length and joined together with a becket bend.

94

Fig. 275: The *Purlin Hitch* is an excellent tie for hoisting horizontal timbers.

Fig. 276: The *Stakeman's Hitch* shown here is used by surveyors, or for any other purpose that requires bundles of stakes to be carried.

Fig. 277: The *Temporary Hitch* is used only as a quick means of fastening a line temporarily. It is not a dependable way to secure a rope that is going to be subjected to a strain.

Plate 29—MISCELLANEOUS HITCHES AND KNOTS

Fig. 278: The *Pin Hitch* shown here is used for belaying a sheet to a belaying pin.

Fig. 279: The *Pin Hitch*, second method, is tied so that the ends are in the reverse direction to the preceding illustration.

Fig. 280: The *Belaying Pin Hitch* can be slacked away gradually when there is a strain on the line.

Fig. 281: The *Racking Hitch* is practically the same as a cat's paw. Two bights are made in a rope, and turned over two times. Then the eyes of both bights are attached to the hook of a block or whatever object they are going to be used with.

Fig. 282 A: The *Cat's Paw* shown here is one of many ways of constructing this knot. The drawn line indicates how the bottom part is brought up over the body of the tie to complete the operation.

B: This shows the finished knot. The short end of the line can be hitched to the standing part to hold the tie secure. Cat's paws are used for attaching a rope to a tackle hook.

Fig. 283: The *Skidder's Hitch* is a way of fastening a chain to small logs for skidding. It is used by lumberjacks in logging camps.

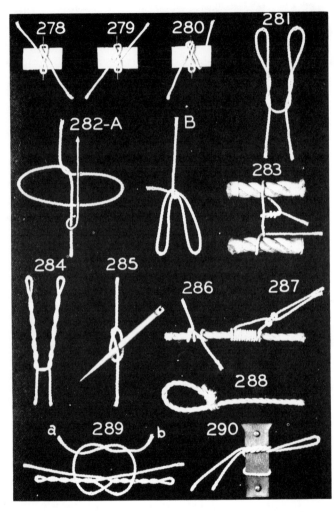

Plate 29—MISCELLANEOUS HITCHES AND KNOTS

Fig. 284: The *Cat's Paw*, second method, is tied the same way as the racking hitch shown in Fig. 281, except that a number of additional twists are usually taken, as illustrated here.

Fig. 285: The *Marlinespike Hitch* is used when leverage is needed, as in heaving a seizing taut. It can be formed very quickly and instantly released. Make a bight in the seizing twine or marline and bring it back over the standing part. Pass the spike over the bight on one side, under the standing part and then over the bight again on the other side.

Fig. 286: The *Well Digger's Hitch* is a form of rolling hitch that is used in connection with the overhaul work on the drum end of a cable, when it is necessary to make fast to a drilling cable in order to support the drill.

Fig. 287: The *Messenger* or *Cable Hitch* is used by linemen for hauling heavy cables. It is formed by placing a half hitch on a cable, and then taking eight or ten turns around the end of the cable. Place another half hitch on the cable after the turns have been made and pull the line taut. Then hitch the two parts of the line together on the hauling end to finish off. This is an effective way to attach a hauling line to a cable, as it forms a very secure tie which holds without slipping.

Fig. 288: The *Pommel Knot* is tied by unlaying the ends of a rope, which are then formed into an overhand knot. After the rope has been bent back on the standing part, and the tie has been secured in the form of a slip eye with the overhand knot worked taut, the knot will appear as shown here. It is used by cowboys to make a lariat fast to the pommel of a saddle.

Fig. 289: *Knotting a Rope-Yarn* is done as follows: clutch the two strands of each rope-yarn together and form a single overhand knot with the two strands, *a* and *b*. (Heavy cord was used here to simplify the illustration.)

The rope-yarn knot is employed when making selvage strops.

Fig. 290: The *Binder Hitch* is handy for securing bags. Its simple formation requires no explanation.

Plate 30—BARREL SLINGS

Fig. 291: The *Vertical Barrel Sling* may be used when a barrel is to be slung in an upright position. It is formed by first placing the barrel upright on the rope. Then join the end and standing part of the rope with an overhand knot above the barrel. Open up the knot, and slip the middle down over the barrel. This will bring half of the knot on each side. Pull both parts of the line up securely and join the end to the standing part with a bowline.

Fig. 292: The *Horizontal Barrel Sling* is also used, at times, for heavy sacks, and therefore is often called a *Sack Sling*.

Fig. 293: The *Butt Sling* is made with an eye splice on one end and two half hitches on the other, after allowing enough slack for a long loop around which a second rope is passed and then secured with a bowline.

Fig. 294: The *Parbuckle Sling* is used as a purchase for raising or lowering heavy casks, guns, etc. When hauling, equal force should be applied to both ends of the rope. A plank is used to form an incline in order to make the leverage more effective.

Fig. 295: The *Vertical Barrel Sling* shown here is made with two overhand knots instead of one as in Fig. 291. This gives both a top and bottom seizing around the barrel and is a very good method to use when extra care and safety are necessary.

Fig. 296: The *Cask Sling* is employed for slinging casks or barrels that have the heads knocked in. It is made by slipping the bight of the rope under the cask and taking

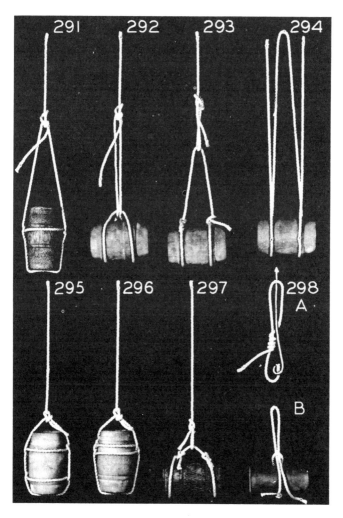

Plate 30—BARREL SLINGS

a hitch with each part over the head. Then the end is joined to the standing part with a bowline.

Fig. 297: The *Hogshead Sling* is used to sling large heavy casks. It is more secure than can hooks or most other slings. Splice an eye in one end of the line. Then take the other end around the cask and through the eye, as in Fig. 293. Next, take the line around the other end of the cask and make it fast with two half hitches, after pulling the connecting part of the line down taut to the cask. It is then seized with a bowline formed in a second line, or a hook, to make fast for lifting.

Fig. 298 A: The *Dutch Sling* is a handy way of forming a tie to sling barrels, spars or any object that is round. The drawn line indicates how the end of the rope is passed through the eye to form the tie.

B: This shows the sling after proper adjustment on a round object.

Plate 31—PACKAGE AND PACK MULE TIES

Fig. 299: The *Packer's Ligature* is used for tying packages and parcels. The illustration needs no explanation.

Fig. 300: The *Bosun's Knot and Half Hitch Package Tie* is another method that is in common use for tying packages. It is simple and easy to duplicate.

Fig. 301: The *Package Tie* shown here is the regular tie used in department stores and elsewhere for tying packages. It is made by first forming a slip eye in the end of the line and bringing it to the center of the package. Pass the line around the package in a horizontal direction, then through the eye, and pull tight. Next, pass the line around the parcel again in a vertical direction, bringing it under the first pass and over its own part, as illustrated. Pull this up tight, and it will hold securely; for added safety it is best to finish off with a half hitch.

100

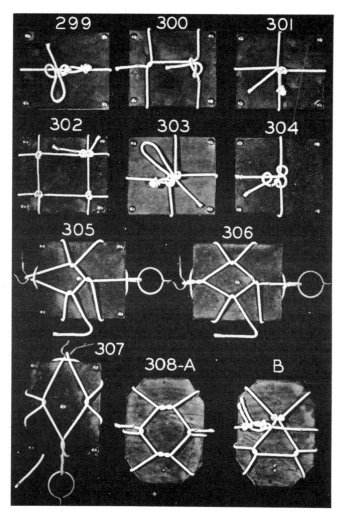

Plate 31—PACKAGE AND PACK MULE TIES

101

Fig. 302: The *Four-Strand Package Tie* shown in this illustration can be followed easily and no explanation as to how it is formed is required.

Fig. 303: The *Stationer's Knot* is also handy for tying up parcels, as it can be made rapidly and can be untied instantly by pulling on the end of the line. First, form a slip eye. Next, pass the line around the parcel in a vertical direction, back through the eye, and pull tight. When this has been done, the line is passed around in a horizontal direction, and passed around the vertical and then the horizontal part. A slip eye is then formed, as shown in the illustration.

Fig. 304: The *Lumber Hitch* shown here can be used for tying up stakes, flooring, bundles of lath, etc. The method of tying is shown clearly in the illustration.

Fig. 305: The *Ranger Hitch* illustrated here is one of several methods that are used for tying packs on animals. It is hardly necessary to describe the tie, as the picture shows "plainer than words" how this tie is formed.

Fig. 306: The *True Diamond Hitch* is shown here in the same form as it was used by the old frontiersmen in the early days of the West. It is still used to a certain extent wherever pack-mule transportation is used, but it is fast fading into memory as a relic of bygone days of the old West. The true diamond hitch can be made fast with an overhand slip eye knot, which also is used for other pack ties.

Fig. 307: The *Lone Jack Diamond* of the western prairie can be thrown by one person, and is tied in the manner illustrated.

Fig. 308 A: The *Old-Time Bedding Hitch* was usually thrown by two packers, one on each side. This picture shows the hitch from underneath.

B: This shows the top side of the hitch after the tie has been completed.

Plate 32—ROPE COILS AND GASKETS

Fig. 309: The *Bulkhead Hitch* shown here is used for suspending rope coils over a peg or any other suitable object. The way the line is done up is quite obvious.

Fig. 310: The *Simple Rope Coil Hitch* shown here is an easy and common method of doing up a line.

Fig. 311: The *Rope Coil Hitch*, second method, is slightly different from the preceding method as can be observed from the illustration.

Fig. 312: To *Flemish Down a Coil of Rope*, the coil must be laid down so that each succeeding fake lies outside of the other. Begin at the center of the coil and work outward, so that each fake lies flat on the deck in a concentric coil. In coiling rope in this manner it is the practice to lay down right-handed rope in a right-hand coil, that is, the rope is laid down from left to right—clockwise, or with the sun. The opposite is the case with left-handed rope. It is laid down from right to left—counterclockwise, or against the sun. In all coils of this type it is important that the running part of the coil be in the center, while the end of the line is on the outside. This is done to insure free running.

Fig. 313: The *Coil Hitch* is used for doing up tackles. It is similar to Fig. 311 except that it has an additional hitch around the eye.

Fig. 314: The *Bulkhead Hitch*, second method. The line is secured to whatever object it is going to be attached to in the manner shown in the illustration.

Fig. 315 A and B: *Making Up a Gasket*. When sails are taken in on sailing vessels, they are lashed to the yards with ropes which are called gaskets. When under sail the gaskets are, of course, not in use and therefore must be coiled up in a fashion that will permit them to be released instantly when it is so desired. A gasket is made

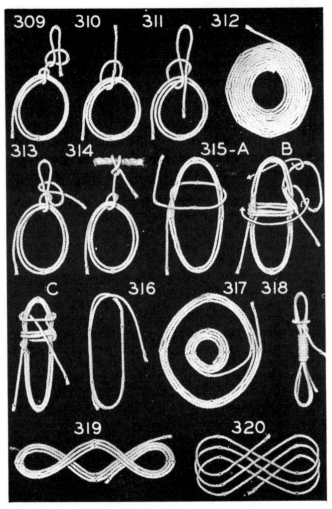

Plate 32—ROPE COILS AND GASKETS

in the following manner: Take the bight of the gasket about four feet from the end which is made fast. Now begin coiling it up in the hand as shown in Fig. 315 A. When the entire line has been coiled, it is flattened out; but be careful that none of the bights in the coil are dropped out of the hand. Next, take several turns around the coil with the standing end. The bight of the standing end is now passed through the upper portion of the coil and then passed over the top of all the bights as shown by the drawn line in Fig. 315 B. The working end in this case is left free in order to make the illustration clear, but in actual use it forms part of the standing end which is made fast.

C: This shows the gasket after the bight has been brought to rest which automatically converts it to inside hitches as it is securely adjusted to make the coil fast.

Fig. 316: To *Coil Down Rope* is to lay it down right-handed or left-handed as the lay of the rope requires, with one fake directly over the fake below it. The coil is then capsized to insure free running.

Fig. 317: To *Flemish Down a Coil of Rope*, second method, as illustrated here, two flat concentric coils are formed with the first or inside coil serving as a heart, around which the rope is then coiled as an outside layer in the manner shown.

Fig. 318: The *Heaving Line* or *Sash Cord Coil* is practically the same as a gasket shortening except that it is started from a lower position near the opposite end and the line is put through the center of the coil at the beginning. The round turns are then taken on top instead of on the bottom of each other as in the gasket method. Otherwise it is finished the same way.

Fig. 319: The *Overlapping Figure-of-Eight Coil* is simply a flemish coil in which two of the opposite sides are overlapped after the coil has been laid down.

Fig. 320: *Faking Down Hawsers* is sometimes done in the manner illustrated. The first step is to lead the line out, removing all kinks and twists. Then begin by winding the rope, at its secured end, in a crisscross manner, each fake being placed directly over the fake below it.

Plate 33—ROPE SHORTENINGS AND SLINGS

Fig. 321: A *Splice in the Standing Part of a Rope*. When making a footrope knot of three strands it is necessary to splice a short piece of marline into the middle of another piece of rope. This splice is placed in the center of the footrope and therefore is not visible.

Fig. 322 A: The *Three-Strand Diamond Footrope Knot* is begun by first tying the diamond knot as shown in Plate 18 Fig. 174. It can then be followed around and either doubled or tripled as desired.

B: This shows the knot with two passes which are drawn up tight and with the ends cut off short to finish. Footrope knots are used on the footropes on the yards of sailing ships to prevent the sailors' feet from slipping.

Fig. 323 A: The *Halter Shortening* is used for doing up halter ropes. This shows how the operation is started with the line turned upside down.

B: This shows the completed shortening. As many turns can be taken as desired.

Fig. 324: The *Twist Braid* is laid out in the same manner as for the halter shortening. The line is then worked back and forth through the other parts in the same way that a three-strand Turk's head is woven, until the required amount of braid has been formed.

Fig. 325 A: The *Regular Sling Shortener* is begun by first laying out the rope as shown. Then bights *a* and *b* are brought together.

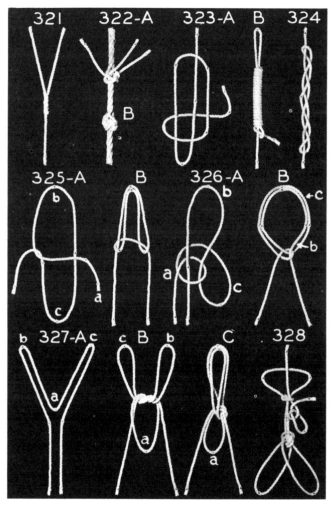

Plate 33—ROPE SHORTENINGS AND SLINGS

B: When this has been done, the two bights may be placed over a hook (although a hook is not shown in the illustration), and the sling is ready to use. The sling can be shortened as much as desired simply by pulling on bights a and b.

Fig. 326 A: The *Longshoreman's Knot* often can be of real service when handling cargo aboard ship, or whenever a sling or strop must be used. It is then sometimes necessary to shorten the sling, but this must be done without tying knots in the rope which might jam if this were attempted. The problem can be solved easily by using one of the various sling-shorteners. To make the knot shown here, first form a loop, a. Bight b is next drawn up through the loop as illustrated. Then parts b and c are brought together.

B: This pictures the finished knot. Bights b and c are now placed on the hook.

Fig. 327 A: The *Regular Sling Shortener*, second method, is begun by dividing the rope into two bights b and c, as illustrated. Next, make an overhand knot, using both bights b and c.

B: This shows the rope after the first stage has been completed. Bights b and c are now brought together and placed on a hook.

C: The completed knot is pictured here. In actual use, loop a hangs free, because the knot itself jams and prevents this slack from being drawn up. This, in fact, is one of the functions of the knot. If the loop were drawn up tight, the knot would be hopelessly jammed.

Fig. 328: A *Diver's Life Line* or *Fireman's Rescue Knot* is an effective means of securing a line around a diver as a safety precaution when he is being lowered into a hatch or other dangerous part of a submerged ship.

Start by tying a double bowline on the bight. Both loops of the bowline are then pulled up over the diver's legs, after which a hitch is taken around his waist with the long end of the line, thus pulling the loops of the bowline up tight in the crotch. Tie a slip knot in the hitch so that it will not pull up tight around the waist and then bring the short end of the line up and pass it under both parts of the eye that forms the slip knot. To finish off, run the end back under its own part and over both parts of the eye in the slip knot.

Plate 34—ROPE LADDER MAKING

Fig. 329: The *Ladder Rung Knot* is tied with two parts of rope. One part is laid out with a bight at each end. The other part is passed through the top bight on the right as shown. Any number of round turns can be taken, suitable to the length of the rung. The rope is then passed through the lower bight on the left, and the knot is pulled taut.

Fig. 330: In the *Rope Ladder* shown here, the rope rungs are made as in Fig. 329. For every other rung, the knot is reversed by forming it the opposite way.

Fig. 331: The *Wall* or *American Shroud Knot* is made as follows: Unlay the rope for a suitable length and marry the ends; then form a wall knot on each side with each set of three strands, the strands going with the lay. The ends are then spliced into the standing part. This type of knot can be formed with any kind of suitable tie such as a diamond, manrope or stopper knot which also are formed back to back in the same way. It was used in the days before the introduction of wire rigging to repair shrouds that had been shot away in action.

Figs. 332 A, B and C: In the *Stern Rope Ladder with Wooden Rungs*, the rungs are always spaced about 12 inches apart. If the ladder is to be from 24 to 25 feet long, it will require about two dozen rungs, each one a

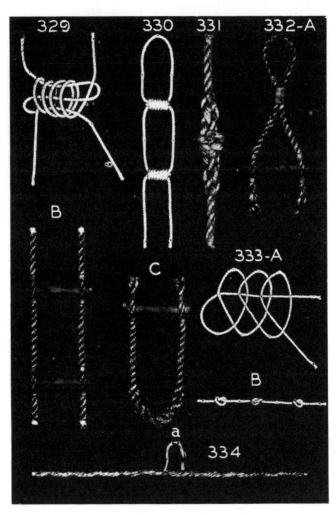

Plate 34—ROPE LADDER MAKING

110

foot long, with the ends scored according to the size of the rope being used. After stretching and laying out the proper amount of rope, middle it and seize it around a thimble. Then mark off on both parts of the rope the place intended for each rung. Beginning at the end nearest the thimble, open the rope up with a fid and push a rung in. Repeat on the opposite side, and continue until all the rungs are placed. Then, using a 7- or 8-turn whipping, seize the rope on both sides just above and below each rung. Splice both the ends together to finish the operation. Fig. 332 A represents the top part, whereas Figs. 332 B and C show the middle and bottom parts respectively. It was necessary to illustrate the ladder in three sections in order to fit the complete operation into the photograph.

Figs. 333 A and B: In the *Trick Chain of Overhand Knots* the hitches are laid out in the fashion shown in Fig. 333 A. Then the end of the line is passed through the hitches and pulled taut, bringing the knots out as they appear in Fig. 333 B.

Fig. 334: *Taking a Rope-Yarn Out of a Strand*. It is surprising how few people know how to execute such a simple operation as taking a rope-yarn out of a strand. The method commonly used is to extract it from the end. The proper method is to grasp the yarn, *a*, from the center of the strand, and then withdraw it.

Plate 35—GENERAL KNOT WORK

Fig. 335: The *Spanish Windlass* is an old device used to exert a drawing force by heaving two ends of a rope together. It is made as shown in the illustration, but two marlinespikes are used instead of the two wooden pins shown at *a*, while *b* represents a steel or stout wooden

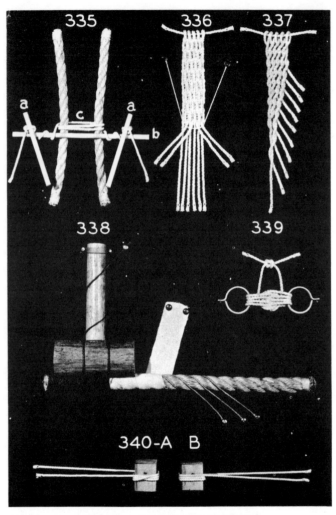

Plate 35—GENERAL KNOT WORK

bar and *c* a well greased line. It is useful when clapping on a throat seizing.

Fig. 336: The *Sword Mat* is formed by first middling the strands over a lashing. Then middle a length of sail twine by passing it between the top and bottom parts of the strand, next to the lashing. Proceed by taking every other strand up across the weave, with the alternate strands laying down, and pass the sail twine, or warp, from each side. Next, bring the bottom strands up, with the top strands laying down, and again pass the warp between the strands as illustrated. Continue this method until the mat is of the desired length and then sew the ends together to finish off. There are various ways to make these mats, differing only in certain details. The old method of using a primitive loom is still frequently followed. But the method described here will be found much quicker and easier. The sword mat is a suitable design for covering sennit frames, etc. Any size line can be used for the work.

Fig. 337: The *Wrought* or *Paunch Mat* is begun by taking any desired number of strands and middling them over a lashing. Next, bring the underneath strand over the top strand of each set from right to left, all the way across. Pass each strand under two strands toward the right side, and back over the same two strands toward the left side. Follow this procedure with each strand in turn, until the weave reaches the required length. The outside strand on each side serves as a filler for attaching the other strands. In this method, it will be noted that the strands are worked down into a point on the left side by tapering the weave from the right side down. This is one of the old-type mats once used for heavy rigging on sailing ships. It also makes an attractive design for covering sennit frames.

Fig. 338: *Worming, Parceling,* and *Serving.* These are

113

the three essential types of work necessary to protect a rope from chafing or from rotting, due to dampness.

Worming consists of laying strands of marline, spunyarn, or other suitable material along the spiral grooves of the rope in the direction of the lay. This is done to fill in the hollow grooves in the rope and to give it a smooth, round appearance.

Parceling is done by wrapping small strips of canvas, usually tarred, around the rope. The canvas strips are wrapped with the lay in overlapping turns. This is done so that the overlapping turns will have a tendency to shed water.

Serving consists of a tight binding of marline or spunyarn around and against the lay of the rope which has previously been wormed and parceled. This work is done with a serving mallet and requires two men. The marline is wrapped around the handle of the serving mallet as illustrated. It is then passed around the rope, two or three turns being made, depending upon how tight the serving is to be. The mallet is passed around the rope, each revolution adding an additional turn to the service as the work proceeds.

Remember the old verse:

> "Worm and parcel with the lay;
> Turn and serve the other way."

Fig. 339: Shows one of the many different types of *Rose Lashings;* it is tied by taking a number of cross turns, as illustrated. Next, pass the line on top down through between the opening and the crosses, while the line underneath is passed up through the same opening. Both lines are then passed around the crosses in opposite directions, forming two or three round turns, after which they are knotted together with a square knot. It is a handy way for seizing two eyes.

114

Figs. 340 A and B: A *Brickmason's* or *Cement Worker's Hitch* is used to make lines fast to rectangular stakes. Fig. 340 A shows the back while Fig. 340 B shows it from the front.

Plate 36—GENERAL KNOT WORK

Fig. 341: The proper way to *Rattle Down*, i.e., secure a ratline to a shroud, is shown in the accompanying illustration. The eyes spliced into the ends of the ratlines are made fast to the shrouds by lashings. These are passed through the eyes as illustrated and after a sufficient number of turns have been taken with the lashing, several cross turns are taken and the ends are secured with a clove hitch. It will be noticed in this connection that the eyes spliced in the ratlines are always secured to the shrouds with the flat surface of the eye facing upward. This eliminates the possibility of rain water lying in the cup on the bottom of the eye.

Fig. 342: The *Midshipman's Hitch* shown here is a variation of the standard method of forming this knot as illustrated in Plate 1, Fig. 14. The author has found that by forming the tie in a slightly different manner, with the working end reversed to come out on the side opposite to that in the former method, the knot is less likely to capsize under a strain, thereby making this tie more dependable.

Fig. 343: The *Anchor Bowline* represents one of the common methods of bending an anchor line to an anchor ring.

Figs. 344 A and B: The *Common Three-Strand Coxcomb* is tied as follows: Seize three strands to a rail or other object; next, take one strand and form a left-handed half hitch. With another strand, form a right-handed half hitch. Then tie a left-handed half hitch. In the illus-

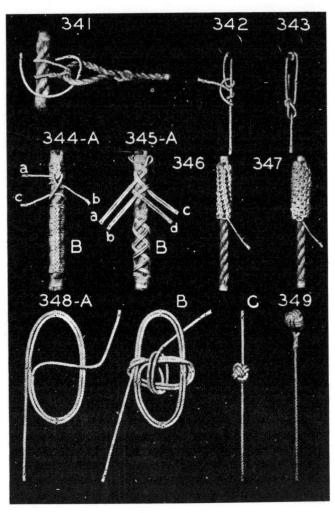

Plate 36—GENERAL KNOT WORK

116

tration, *a* has been half-hitched to the left, *b* to the right, and *c* to the left. The next step is to begin with *a* again, hitching it to the right this time. The complete coxcomb is shown in Fig. 344 B.

Figs. 345 A and B: The *Four-Strand Coach Whipping* or *Cross-Pointing* is tied by the same method as a round sennit braid. In addition to its use as a braided line, it can also be formed around a core, as a covering for a stanchion, telescope, rope point, etc. It can be made with any even number of strands, which are often doubled, trebled or quadrupled. To begin, take strand *c* and lay it across strand *a*. Strand *b* is brought around over *c* and under *d*, toward the opposite side. Follow up by bringing strand *a* around under *c* and over *d* to its own side. Then bring strand *c* around under *b* and over *a* to its own side —and so on, until the desired number of passes has been made. Fig. 345 A shows how the seizings are made to start, and Fig. 345 B shows the coach-whipping completed.

Fig. 346: The *Open Fender Hitching* is the method of hitching used to cover large fenders, such as those on the bow of a tugboat; a familiar sight to everyone. This type of hitching is done with one strand. To begin, take two complete turns around the work with the end of the strand. Take the other end and begin half-hitching on these two turns until you have gone completely around the fender or rope. The next half hitch is taken on the bight, between two of the first group of half hitches that has been made. This is continued until the desired length is reached. It will be found necessary, when covering a large fender, to add a length of line from time to time; this can be accomplished by long-splicing the two ends together. When working on an irregular surface a half hitch can be left out or can be added at intervals, which- ever may be necessary.

Fig. 347: The *Closed Fender Hitching* is made in the

117

same way as the hitching in Fig. 346. The hitches are taken much closer together, however, so that the core upon which the work is being done can barely be seen through the hitching, and the form of hitching is inverted or opposite from the preceding method.

Figs. 348 A, B and C: The *Monkey Fist* is a type of knot used to put weight on the end of a heaving line. To make it, form two or three loops (usually three). Two are used here for the sake of clarity in the illustration. After forming the two loops as shown in Fig. 348 A, pass the end around the first set of loops; take two more turns, and pass the end through the first set of loops and around the second set of loops, as shown in Fig. 348 B. Then take two more turns, as before, and pull up tight. Care should be taken in working this knot up taut, in order to get the proper shape. Fig. 348 C shows the knot as it looks when pulled up.

Fig. 349: The *Three-Strand Monkey Fist* is the regular form of monkey fist used for heaving lines. It is made by taking three turns instead of two, but is otherwise tied in the same way as in Fig. 348.

Plate 37—BOATSWAIN'S CHAIR AND LASHINGS

Fig. 350: The *Crowned Monkey Fist* has a series of spiral crowns worked around a core and then finished off with a spritsail sheet weave on top, which is nothing more than bringing one outside strand from each side toward the opposite side, or in other words laying them parallel to each other but leading in opposite directions. The side strands are then alternately tucked over and under the cross strands in order to close the weave up.

Fig. 351: *Tricing in Two Ropes* is done in the following manner: A short piece of line is made fast to one of the two ropes and then several turns are taken around both of them as illustrated. Pull all of the slack out of the two ropes by hauling on the free end of the lashing and then secure one end of the latter to either of the ropes with a clove hitch.

Fig. 352: A *Spiral Fender,* sixteen inches in length and two and one-half inches in diameter, requires three fathoms of three-quarter-inch rope. It is made in the following manner: The first step is to middle the rope and then clap on a stout seizing to form a small eye. Next, unlay all the strands and whip the end of each. Take the strands and form a continuous series of crowns in one direction; continue these crowns until the fender is about eighteen inches in length. Do not pull the crowns up taut, but as they are made, merely take out the slack. Next, pass a stout piece of twine up through the center of the fender. All of the six strands of the rope are then attached to this piece of twine and are pulled up inside the crowns, after which each one of the strands is pulled out separately through the six openings just below the seizing. Then, with the use of a fid, proceed to draw the slack out of the crowns until the entire fender has been drawn up as tight as possible. Pull the ends of the strands out until they are drawn up tightly and cut them off short below the seizing. The method shown here is finished off with a spritsail sheet weave for convenience of presentation.

Fig. 353: *Rigging for a Boatswain's Chair* is shown in the accompanying illustration. After the gantline has been rove through the block and secured to the chair bridle as shown and the workman has been hauled up, he places the hauling part of the rope in front of him, grasps a bight and draws it through the bridle. The line is then passed over the workman's head and body, down under the chair and up in front of him again as shown

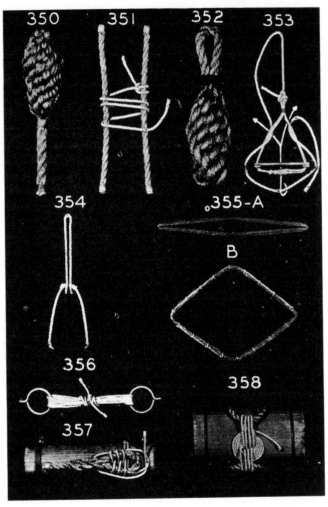

Plate 37—BOATSWAIN'S CHAIR AND LASHINGS

by the arrow. All of the slack is hauled out of the line and it is then secured. To lower the chair, all that is necessary is to slack off on the knot and allow the line to run out.

Fig. 354: The *Bale Sling* shows the proper method of passing a strop on a bale or sack.

Figs. 355 A and B: The *Selvagee Strop* is stronger than a spliced strop of the same number of yarns. It is usually made of small line (marline, rope-yarns, spun-yarn) or of rope, warped around two spikes which are spaced the desired distance apart. When enough turns have been made, the ends are square-knotted together and temporary seizings placed on the strop. Its entire length is then lashed with marline hitching.

Fig. 356: A *Wedding Lashing* is used to join the two eyes which have been previously made in the ends of two ropes. The lashing line is passed successively through the eyes a number of times, after which the ends of the lashing are passed down between the turns and a number of additional turns is taken over the body of the lashing, the ends of the lashing line being passed in opposite directions. The ends are finally secured with a square knot in the center, as shown.

Fig. 357: The *Rose Lashing* shown here was used on sailing ships to lash the footropes to the yards. It can also be used to lash an eye to a spar as illustrated. The method of tying the knot is self-explanatory.

Fig. 358: Another form of *Rose Lashing*. It is used to secure a rope with eyes spliced into each end around a mast or spar. A lanyard is spliced through one eye and then passed in figure-of-eight fashion over and back under one eye, then over and back under the other. This process is continued until a sufficient number of turns have been made. The end is then taken round and round in coil fashion between the cross turns, as shown.

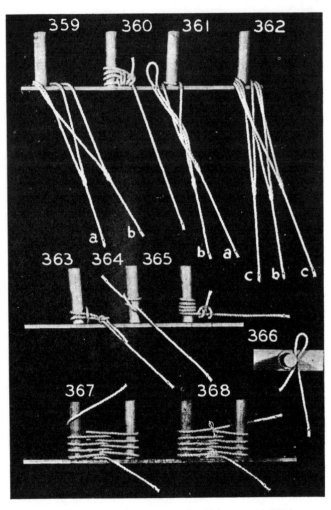

Plate 38—METHODS OF SECURING HAWSERS

Plate 38—METHODS OF SECURING HAWSERS

Fig. 359: *Placing Hawsers Over a Bollard* on a dock should be done in such a manner that no matter how many hawsers are used, each can be removed or cast off without interfering with the others. This is done in the following manner: Assume that the bight of the hawser marked *a* was placed over the bollard first, then when the second hawser *b* is passed, its bight is brought up through the bight of hawser *a*, as illustrated. If the bight of hawser *b* were not brought up through that of *a*, it would not be possible to cast off hawser *a* without first releasing hawser *b*, which would not in all cases be desirable.

Fig. 360: The *Single Chain Fastening* is used over a single pile in the water. It consists of a series of figure-of-eight turns taken around the pile and over the standing part of the line, after which the end is secured with two half hitches.

Fig. 361: *Securing a Hawser on a Bollard with a Round Turn*. It occasionally happens that when a hawser is passed over a bollard it is given a round turn such as is indicated with the hawser *a* in the accompanying illustration. When this is the case, the hawser would not run free when cast off, as it would in the case shown in Fig. 359. To prevent such an occurrence the bight of the second hawser *b* is rove through the bight of hawser *a*, as shown, before being put over the pile. Either of the two hawsers can then be cast off without interfering with the other.

Fig. 362: *Three Hawsers on One Bollard*. It is sometimes necessary to pass three or more hawsers over the same bollard. If this is done the bight of each line (*a*, *b* and *c*) must pass up through the eyes of all of the others, as shown in the illustration. By performing the

123

operation in this manner any single line may be cast free.

Fig. 363: The *Lark's Head Mooring Hitch* is another simple method for securing a mooring line to a pile.

Fig. 364: The *Clove Hitch Mooring* is used for the same purpose as that in the example above.

Fig. 365: The *Round Turn Mooring Hitch* is made by passing several turns around a pile after which the end is made secure with two half hitches.

Fig. 366: The *Slippery Hitch* is a knot that should always be used on the sheets of small sailboats. One pull on the end will release the sheet. This is often desirable when a sudden puff of wind hits the sail and there is danger that the boat might capsize.

Fig. 367: *Securing a Mooring Line,* first method. This is a means of securing a mooring line with a series of figure-of-eight turns about a pair of bitts. The end of the line may be half-hitched to one of the bitts or it may be seized as shown in Fig. 368.

Fig. 368: *Securing a Mooring Line,* second method. This illustration is the same as Fig. 367, except that the end of the line is shown seized to prevent its running out. A seizing such as this is always applied when wire rope is used.

Plate 39—A STAGE SLING AND BELAYING PIN TIES

Fig. 369 A: The *Stage Sling* is a rope design often found very useful by sailors. When working over the side of a ship or in a shipyard, it is frequently necessary to have a light yet sturdy scaffold capable of supporting one or two men. This need can be served by what is known as a stage, consisting of a long flat plank with two "horns," bolted at right angles to the plank. The purpose of these horns is to keep the plank away from the surface being worked on. In order to suspend the stage from—let us say—a ship's side, it must be rigged with ropes. This is done as follows: first, lay out the rope as shown, into a marlinespike hitch. This is made a short distance from the end.

B: Next place the knot under the horn, bring part *a* over the top of the stage. Bights *b* and *c* are then brought over and on top of the horns on each side.

C: The end is now brought up and a bowline formed, using the end and the standing part as indicated. But, before drawing the knot taut, be certain that both parts are even, so that the stage will not be canted when it hangs on the rope. One of these knots is made on each horn. The standing parts may be rove through the blocks on the deck above, with the ends brought down and made fast to the stage. This eliminates climbing back up on deck to lower the stage—which would be necessary if it were made fast to a railing.

Fig. 370: The *Heaving Line Bowline* is another knot of great usefulness to seafaring men. When docking a ship and sending the hawsers ashore, the operation must, as a rule, be carried out as quickly as possible. After the heaving line has been cast ashore, there is usually a good deal of unnecessary fumbling in making the end fast to the eye of the hawser. This can be eliminated by tying a bowline, using the method illustrated here. The end of the line is first rove through the eye of the hawser. Then take the standing part of line *a* in the left hand, and place it in the position shown. End *b*, which is in the right hand, is next passed under the middle strand as shown by the arrow. Now cast end *b* away from you, and at the same time give standing part *a* a sharp jerk. The knot will automatically fall into a bowline. Al-

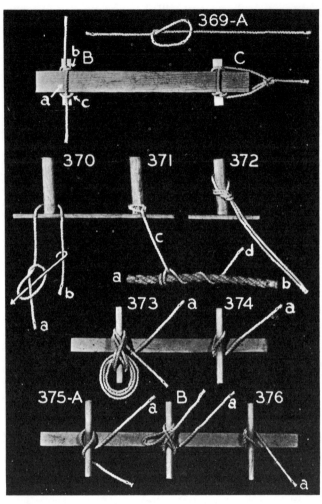

Plate 39—A STAGE SLING AND BELAYING PIN TIES

though this method appears to be a bit drawn out, a little practice will enable anyone to tie the knot in half the time required to tie a bowline in the ordinary manner. This method can be used also when making fast to a pile (as in the illustration), or in any other situation where a bowline is advisable.

Fig. 371: The *Stopper* may be applied when tying up a ship, or when a heavy load is to be suspended and it is desired to take the rope off the niggerhead or capstan. End *a* is the part leading to the capstan, and standing part *b* leads to the load. The stopper, *c*, is made fast to the bitts and secured to the working line with a stopper hitch, the end being "dogged" with the lay, and the bitter end *d* held in the hand. End *a* is next slacked off the capstan until the stopper is bearing all the strain. Then make end *a* fast to the bitts or chock, whichever is used, and remove the stopper to complete the operation.

Fig. 372: The *Overhand Wharf Tie* is an easy method of making a line fast to a pile on a dock when only the bight of the line is available. A simple overhand knot is first made in such a way that when the operation has been completed the bight will face upward. All that then remains is to cast the bight over the top of the pile.

Fig. 373: *Coiling Rope on a Belaying Pin.* This is the correct method for coiling the end of a rope on a belaying pin. When a considerable amount of rope remains left over after the rope has been belayed, the remainder is then coiled up in the hand and when near the end, the coil is placed against the pinrail and several more turns are taken on the belaying pin. This uses up the remaining end and also secures the coil as illustrated; *a* is the standing part.

Fig. 374: The *Correct Method of Belaying an Eye-Spliced Line.* When the standing part of the rope leads from above, the end is brought around in back of the belaying pin, beneath the pinrail, and then the eye is placed over the top of the belaying pin.

Figs. 375 A and B: *Belaying a Line to a Belaying Pin* is done as shown. The rope is first brought around the pin, then up and around the top of it, after which a number of figure-of-eight turns are taken around the line and the pin; *a* represents the standing part. When enough turns have been taken, the end is finished off with a slippery hitch illustrated in Fig. 375 B.

Fig. 376: *Another Method of Making an Eye Fast to a Belaying Pin*. When the standing part *a* leads from below, the end is first brought around the top of the belaying pin, and the eye is passed over the bottom of the pin to finish.

Plate 40—VARIOUS TYPES OF POLE LASHINGS

Fig. 377: *Poles Lashed and Wedged* in the manner shown in this illustration are held securely, with little likelihood of their slipping or working loose. After the lashings have been applied, small wooden wedges are driven between them and the poles as shown. This tends to take up any slack in the lashings.

Fig. 378: The *Putlog Lashing* is employed to lash two square timbers together. The manner in which it is formed is clearly shown in the illustration.

Fig. 379: The *Telegraph Hitch* is used to hoist long poles or piles in a vertical position. To make the hitch, take a piece of line of sufficient length, middle it, and make cross turns around the pole as shown. A short bar is then placed under the final cross turn and a turn is taken about it, after which the ends of the rope are secured with a reef knot, forming a bight for the hoisting hook.

Fig. 380: The *Double Chain Lashing* shows the man-

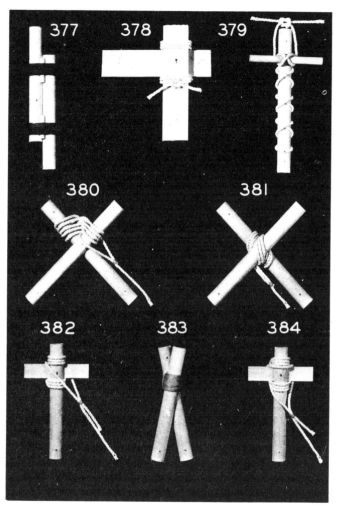

Plate 40—VARIOUS TYPES OF POLE LASHINGS

ner of making a line fast to a pair of crossed shears. The end is seized to the standing part of the rope after a sufficient number of turns have been taken about the shears.

Fig. 381: A *Loop Lashing* such as that shown, illustrates the manner in which the bight of a hawser is made fast to a pair of crossed shears. The bight of the hawser is passed over, under, and around the legs of the shears in the manner shown, after which the loop of the bight is placed over the top of one of the legs, leaving the standing part of the hawser as shown.

Fig. 382: The *Crossed Lashing* is another method used to make a line fast on the head of a pair of crossed shears. Any number of turns may be taken as shown, each one being crossed in back, after which the end of the lashing is made fast to its standing part with a seizing.

Fig. 383: The *Shear Head Lashing* is used to lash the heads of a pair of shears together. The shears are laid parallel to each other on the ground; a number of turns are taken around them, after which several cross turns are taken. The ends are then finished off with a reef knot.

Fig. 384: The *Square Lashing* shown in this illustration is used for much the same purpose as that shown in Fig. 382. It is made in the same manner except that the turns are parallel and not crossed.

Plate 41—ROPE POINTING, FLEMISH AND SPINDLE EYES

Fig. 385 A: The *Common Rope Pointing* is one of the best methods of finishing off the end of a rope to prevent the strands from fraying. It also stiffens the end of the rope so that it can be passed through a block easily. To start the work, clap a stout seizing on the rope about ten inches back from its end. Unlay the strands and make enough nettles to cover the rope completely. These nettles are shown in the illustration at *a*. There should always be an even number of nettles; in this case, twelve. The remaining yarns are then tapered by scraping, after which they are marled together securely, as shown at *b*. Next, pass each alternate nettle down and the remainder up, laying the latter along the conical center. At the point where the two groups of nettles separate, take two turns around the upright nettles and the cone with a piece of marline, securing the second turn with a half hitch. Next, bring the vertical nettles down on the standing part of the rope and the other nettles up along the center. The marline is again brought up and two turns taken about the now vertical nettles and the cone, after which the last turn of the marline is again secured with a half hitch. Repeat this sequence of operations until the desired length has been reached. A blood knot can also be used with marline instead of a half hitch to stop the nettles around the core as this form of tie holds hard and fast for an operation of this nature, and it is probably more secure than a half hitch.

B: Do not stop all of the nettles to the work in order to finish it off, but take three loose turns around the one set of nettles and the core. Next, take each nettle from the second group and bring it up over the turns of marline and then back underneath them as shown at *d*. The nettles shown at *c* have not been tucked. When all of the nettles of the second group have been tucked as explained, the turns of the marline are brought up taut. All of the ends of the nettles are cut off and the work will look as shown in Fig. 385 C. The core has been purposely left intact in this illustration to make the work easier to understand, but in actual practice it is also cut off after working the point down as far as possible.

Fig. 386: Represents an *Ordinary Eye Pointing*. Form

131

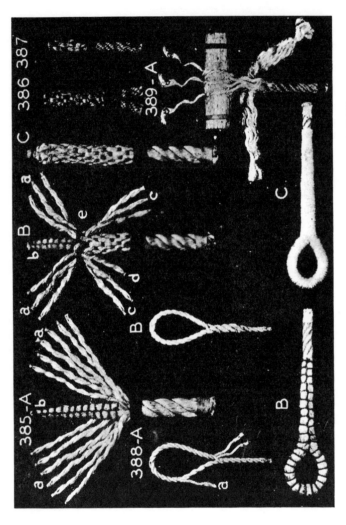

Plate 41—ROPE POINTING, FLEMISH AND SPINDLE EYES

the eye and place a seizing around the two parts of rope, then unlay the strands and select the outside yarns which are laid back and tied to the body of the rope. Taper the strands forming the heart and marl them down in the usual manner. Make two round turns with marline to start the pointing, after laying each alternate pair of yarns back and the others down. Continue with another pair of round turns, bringing each alternate pair of yarns down and the others back with each additional pass. Make a secure whipping on the end to finish the job.

Fig. 387: An *Ordinary Rope Pointing* done in the same manner as the work illustrated in Fig. 386.

Fig. 388 A: The *Flemish Eye Splice,* which is a little different from the common eye splice, can be used when there is a tendency for the eye to spread apart. First, unlay the rope a sufficient length for turning in a common eye splice. Select one of the three strands and unlay it until the remaining two strands are long enough to form an eye of the desired size. Bend these two strands down until they meet the single strand, *a*, again. Instead of laying strand *a* up on the standing part, lay it in the other direction, beginning a short distance from the end of the opening strands.

B: When strand *a* has been laid up again, proceed to dispose of the ends as in the common splice. In this illustration the strands were tucked by using the sailmaker's method which brings the strands through the rope and along the lay in a uniform manner.

Figs. 389 A, B and C: An *Artificial* or *Spindle Eye in Four-Strand Manila Rope.* Place a whipping at a distance from the end of the rope about equal to three times the rope's circumference. Unlay the strands back as far as the whipping and separate them into yarns, which are to be divided into two equal groups. There are two ways in which this eye can be formed. The yarns can be either knotted together or they can be laid up into nettles and then knotted together around a spar having a diameter equal to twice the circumference of the rope. Take care not to make all of the overhand knots, or double overhand knots for added security, at one place around the spar, instead, space them equally distant from each other. After all of the yarns have been knotted together, lay them down around the eye and on the standing part of the rope. Next, take a length of marline and bind the knotted yarns with marline hitches all around the eye. Scrape and taper the ends of the yarns down on the standing part of the rope and marl them in the same manner as the eye. The eye and the standing part are then served, or the eye can be parceled before serving, to make a neat job. Fig. 389 A shows the first stage of the work, and Fig. 389 B as it looks when marled. Fig. 389 C shows the completed eye.

This type of eye is used for the collars of stays and was used also for the lower end of manropes when the lanyard was spliced in back.

Plate 42—NET MAKING AND MESHING

Fig. 390: The *Rope Cargo Net* is usually made of three-strand rope although four-strand is occasionally used. The size of the rope varies according to the type and weight of material to be handled. It is customary to make the frame (the rope running around the outer edge of the net into which the mesh ropes are spliced) of heavier rope than the mesh.

To begin, take a length of rope and longsplice the ends together in such a manner as to make a frame the proper size when the splice is completed. Next, cut the mesh ropes, leaving about one and one-half feet over the frame on each side. First splice in all the vertical mesh ropes. The ends are spliced into the frame after the mesh rope is tucked under one, and back around, two strands. The common eye splice is used. Take a horizontal mesh rope and splice it into the frame. Then unlay one strand from this rope until it has been unlaid down to the first vertical mesh rope nearest the eye. This strand is then tucked under one strand of the vertical mesh rope. Next lay the strand up again until it reaches the next mesh rope. The single strand is then tucked under one strand of this rope again. Proceed to lay the rope up again until the next mesh rope is reached. This process is repeated until the opposite frame rope is reached. The mesh rope is then laid up completely, tucked under one, and then back around two strands in the frame rope, and spliced.

This procedure is carried out until all the horizontal mesh ropes have been spliced in place. The rope forming the inverted "V" at the top of the net, which is called a becket, is spliced into the frame rope in each corner. (This rope is not tucked under one and around two strands but passed completely around the frame rope instead.) Another such becket is spliced into the lower end of the net. These are placed over a cargo hook and serve as a means of lifting the net.

Fig. 391: To start a *Fish Net* such as that shown here, string up a length of cord and secure the end of the netting twine to the cord by means of a clove hitch. Any kind of netting needle or shuttle can be used that will perform the job properly. Commercial needles are usually $6\frac{1}{2}$ to 8 inches long; $\frac{5}{8}$ to $\frac{7}{8}$ inch wide, and approximately $\frac{1}{8}$ inch thick. The needle is filled by clove hitching the end of the twine around the central spine and leading it up the other side. Then bend the spine until its point projects just enough to permit the twine to be looped over the spine. The twine is then led back through the groove

135

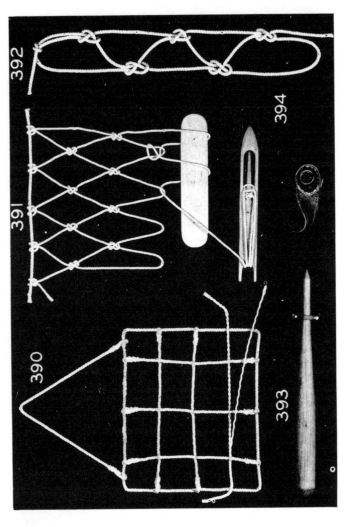

Plate 42—NET MAKING AND MESHING

at the base of the needle to the starting side, where the process is repeated. The needle should be filled until the twine is approximately ¼ inch from the end of the spine. Leave about 24 inches of twine not wound on the needle. Then continue by using a meshing gauge, or stick, to measure the exact length and size of each successive mesh after tying a clove hitch to the foundation cord each time a new mesh is formed. This process is repeated, working from left to right, until the required width of the net is reached. Starting back from right to left, begin forming sheet bends in the bottom of each mesh with a meshing shuttle, which is employed in connection with a meshing gauge of the proper size in order to insure meshes of uniform proportion as shown in the illustration. As the work progresses each knot is pulled taut and rows of meshes are worked back and forth until the net has reached the required size. If desired, the whole net can be turned over after each new row of meshes has been formed. The operation is thereby simplified so as to keep netting in one direction; either from left to right or vice versa. Note how the meshing shuttle is brought around the meshing gauge and then up underneath, and out through, each succeeding mesh after the sheet bend has been formed. It is then carried around and underneath the mesh with one hand, while holding the bottom of the mesh with the thumb and forefinger of the other hand. The meshing twine is then flipped over the shuttle as it is pulled through in order to form a new knot. Eighteen-thread medium lay seine twine is the most commonly used line for making fish nets.

Fig. 392: *Hammock Making* involves the use of a netting needle and a mesh stick such as are used in weaving nets. The width of the mesh stick determines the size of the mesh in the netting or web of the hammock, and at the same time it keeps all of the meshes the same size;

that is, a mesh stick two inches wide will form a mesh one inch square. The netting needle carries the cord of which the hammock or net is made. It serves as a shuttle for interweaving the cord and for tying the knots. It should be of such size that after being wound with cord it will pass easily through a mesh of the net. Netting meshes are shown in this illustration, but with all of the knots forming them tied loosely. A chain of about fifty such meshes are required for a hammock. After the first chain has been completed the slip eye used to form the first mesh may be untied, making all of the meshes of uniform size and shape. The next step is to open the chain and then turn the mesh over, working another row of meshes back across and into the first row. This process of turning the net over and successively weaving additional rows of meshes is continued until the hammock is the desired width.

Fig. 393: A *Fid* such as that shown here is a tapered piece of hard wood used for separating the strands of a rope in making splices.

Fig. 394: A *Palm* is used primarily in sewing and mending sails and canvas. It is a leather strap worn over the hand, to which is attached a metal plate placed so as to fit into the palm of the sailor's hand.

Plate 43—HAMMOCK CLEWS AND GROMMET EYELETS

Fig. 395: The *Hammock Clews* shown here are formed in the following way: First measure off the desired length for the twelve bights, which are inserted through the grommet eyelets and then attached to the canvas hammock by means of a jackstay. In order to get the same uniform length in each bight, space twelve nails or screws

138

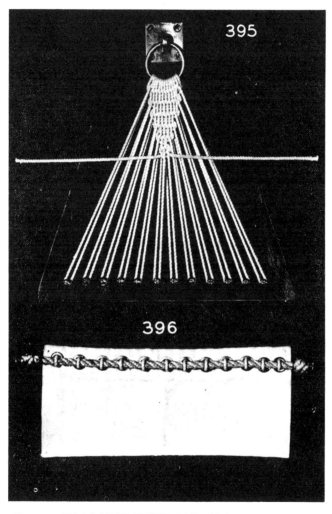

395

396

Plate 43—HAMMOCK CLEWS AND GROMMET EYELETS

139

an equal distance apart and the same length from the hammock ring. Then begin by placing a bight around the outside nail or screw with one end of the line hanging free after being run through the ring. The other end of the line is now run back and forth between the ring and the screws until all twelve screws are covered with bights. After this operation is completed the working end of the line is run through the ring in the opposite manner or vice versa to the side where the operation was started. One end of the line will now be running through the ring from underneath, whereas the other end will be running through from the top. Separate the strands with a rule which can be used as a spreader by passing it, first over one strand, and then under the next, thus bringing one strand up and the next strand down, as in a sword mat. After the spreader has been passed all the way through, the outside strands are used as a filler by running them through behind the spreader and jamming them up snugly into place. This same operation is continued until six passes of the filler strands have been made, being careful to drop a bight on each side after every pass, until the end is reached. When the spreader is run through to separate the strands after each pass with the fillers has been made, caution should be used in picking up the proper strands, as the strands that are up should be dropped down, and the strands that are down should be picked up. After the last pass has been made, a square knot is tied between the two center bights in the manner indicated, to finish the operation.

Fig. 396: Shows how the twelve bights are attached to the jackstay after having been passed through the grommet eyelets on the edge of the canvas. Heavy canvas is used for the construction of the hammock, which can be any length and breadth desired, with about two inches allowed for seams.

140

Plate 44—STEPS IN MAKING A SEA BAG

Figs. 397 A to I: A *Sea Bag*, such as that shown here in the various stages of its construction, is more or less a relic of the bygone days of sailing ships. Some of those used by sailors years ago were of tremendous size, holding all a man's worldly possessions, such as clothing, bedding, dishes, tools of his trade and many other articles which he carried with him from ship to ship and from port to port. Today, however, the once well-known "duffel bag" is rarely seen along the waterfronts of the world. In their stead sailors are using the more conventional types of luggage. However, a sea bag is still very handy aboard ship for the storage of many articles, and those now in use are made in sizes suitable for the purpose for which they are intended. Most of them are made about one foot in diameter and three feet in length. No. 2 canvas is the material used, or for a lighter bag, No. 7 or No. 8 canvas can be used. To make a bag of the size mentioned requires a piece of canvas of the weight desired, 36 inches wide by 42 inches long.

In the working of canvas, it will be noticed, as it is unrolled from the bolt, that there are two colored threads woven into each strip, about one inch from each selvage edge. These are intended as guide lines or markers in sewing the strips together. The strips are so overlapped that the edges of both coincide with these colored threads. Then, no matter whether the seam is made by hand or with a machine, the stitches are taken near the edge of each strip of canvas, using both the edge and the colored threads as guides. After a row of stitches has been made along one edge of the canvas, the material is turned over and a second row of stitches is taken along the other edge of the material, thus making an overlapping flat seam. If the material is wide enough, only one seam may be

141

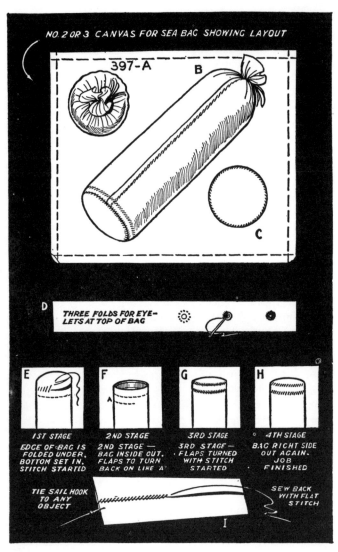

NO. 2 OR 3 CANVAS FOR SEA BAG SHOWING LAYOUT

397-A

B

C

D THREE FOLDS FOR EYE-
LETS AT TOP OF BAG

E
1ST STAGE
EDGE OF BAG IS
FOLDED UNDER.
BOTTOM SET IN.
STITCH STARTED

F
2ND STAGE
2ND STAGE —
BAG INSIDE OUT.
FLAPS TO TURN
BACK ON LINE 'A'

G
3RD STAGE
3RD STAGE -
FLAPS TURNED
WITH STITCH
STARTED

H
4TH STAGE
BAG RIGHT SIDE
OUT AGAIN.
JOB
FINISHED

TIE SAIL HOOK
TO ANY
OBJECT

SEW BACK
WITH FLAT
STITCH

I

Plate 44—STEPS IN MAKING A SEA BAG

needed, but when narrow canvas is used it is frequently necessary to join two cloths, making two such seams, one on each side of the bag.

After the work of forming the sides of the bag has been completed, the next step is to make the top of the bag. This is done by folding one edge of the tubular sack back over itself twice, thus making a seam of three thicknesses. This is sewed down by taking a row of stitches around the bag about one and one-half inches from the top edge. A flat stitch is used in the seam.

The next step is to form the eyelets for the draw cords. These are placed in the seam at the top of the bag, making as many as required by the size of the bag. The first step in making the eyelets it to punch holes through the material, slightly smaller than the desired size of the finished eyelet. Place several turns of sail twine inside each of the holes, in the form of grommets, and proceed to sew them into place. Make two complete turns of stitches around each eyelet, overlapping the stitches the second time around to make a neat job.

The final operation is to attach the bottom to the bag. There is a definite method of determining the size of the material needed for the bottom of the bag. The first step is to lay the tubular section of the bag out flat, then fold it so that there will be three equal folds. In other words, the width of the folded bag will be equal to one-third of the bag when it is laid out flat. In the case of the bag being described, this will be about six inches; this amount is now doubled which makes twelve inches. Then, allowing about one half-inch for a seam all around the bottom, proceed to cut out a circular piece of canvas thirteen inches in diameter. Make a pencil mark around this circular piece about three-quarters of an inch in from its outer circumference. This line is intended as a marker or guide in sewing the bottom in the bag.

Next, turn the tubular section of the bag inside out and

fold the bottom edge back upon itself, making a pencil mark around the edge of the fold as a guide or marker for placing the bottom in its correct position. Match the guide line on the bottom material with that on the tubular section and proceed to sew the bottom on the bag. It should be understood that the outside edge of the bottom will be inside the bag when the work is finished. If desired, another seam may be made around the outer edge of the bottom of the bag after the bottom has been attached, but before the bag is turned right side out. This is not necessary but it adds to the strength of the bottom seam.

Finish off the work by running a drawstring of suitable size through the eyelets.

Plate 45—STITCHES USED IN SEWING CANVAS

Fig. 398: A *Cringle Made Around a Thimble*. Reeve the end of an unlaid strand through the eyelet holes in the sail, then lay the strand up on itself, around the thimble and through the eyelet holes again. Continue by laying both ends up a second time until they meet on top of the thimble. Work the strands taut with a marlinespike, taper the ends and tuck them over one and under one as in splicing, making the last tuck on the inside and under the thimble. Cut the ends off short to finish.

Another method, slightly different, is to unlay a rope the required size of the cringle, then whip the ends and reeve the end of the strand through the eyelet hole on the left side, leaving one end of the strand about a third longer than the other; be sure that the roping of the sail is facing you during this operation. If a thimble is desired in the cringle, lay up the three parts of the strand together. This is done by starting with the short end of the strand toward you, then reeve the long end of the strand away from you and through the eyelet hole on the right side. Pass it through the cringle, which will bring it into the proper place for laying up in the space that is still vacant. When this is completed, one end will be inside the eyelet hole on the right and the other end will be outside the eyelet hole on the left. The ends are next rove through their respective eyelet holes, then over the leech rope and under their own parts, in the form of a hitch. This will bring one hitch out toward you, while the other hitch will come out away from you. Next bring the ends down under one strand on the right and two strands on the left of the cringle nearest it, and proceed by tucking the ends under the two strands nearest the hitch. Fid the cringle out and put the thimble in on the fore-part of the sail. Tuck the ends of the strand back in alternating fashion, heaving them taut. They are then whipped and cut short.

A cringle is finished off on the crown. However, instead of forming a hitch with the ends, they are rove through their respective eyelet holes and are then tucked back under two strands of the cringle, and laid up again to the crown, forming a four-stranded cringle. Finish off by tucking the ends under two strands, then cross them under the crown of the cringle and trim the ends.

Fig. 399: *Hand-Worked Eyelets.* The modern eyelet is made of brass which is set in the canvas with a steel punch. The old-fashioned hand-worked eyelets were much stronger and better for use as reef cringles, because they would not chafe or pull out under a heavy strain. Mark the location for placing the eyelets, and then punch circular holes through the canvas near the roping. These holes should be a trifle smaller than the desired size of eyelet. Next, make a two- or three-strand grommet with a yarn of marline and stretch the grommet over a fid to

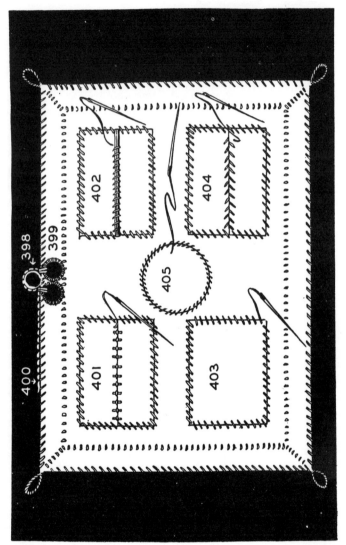

398
399
400
401
402
403
404
405

146

make it hard and round. Proceed to sew the eyelet with a needle threaded with two parts of twisted and waxed heavy sail twine. Sew all around the grommet and through the canvas in circular fashion, keeping each stitch well back from the edge of the hole in the canvas. To finish off, stick the end of a fid through the hole and stretch the eyelet, making it round.

Fig. 400: *Sewing Boltropes to a Sail or Awning.* Place the rope along the edge of the canvas and pick up one strand with each successive stitch, the length of each stitch being governed by the size of the strands in the rope. Boltropes are often sewn to the selvage edge of canvas, but when sewn to a raw edge, the edges must first be folded under, and the rope sewed on so that it covers the raw edge.

Fig. 401: A *Herringbone Stitch* that is used on painted or very stiff canvas. Bring the needle across the opening at each pass, and then through from the opposite side and out toward the middle. Next cross over the stitch, and then stick the needle through from the inside, and out through the side the stitch was started from.

Fig. 402: A *Round Stitch,* which is used to join two edges together, or for quick repair work on heavy canvas. It is made by holding the two edges together and passing the needle through both pieces at right angles to the canvas.

Fig. 403: A *Flat Stitch on a Square Patch.* It is the most common method of sewing two pieces of canvas together. The stitch is made by lapping two pieces of canvas and pushing the needle through the lower piece and up through the edge of the canvas to be joined. When sewing on a patch, be sure to smooth the edges of the parts that are folded under, to make a neat-looking job. To finish off a stitch, take about two turns around the needle and pull up taut, then cut short.

Fig. 404: A *Baseball Stitch* is used for sewing up rips in canvas where a snug fit is required.

Fig. 405: A *Flat Stitch on a Round Patch*. This is the same type of stitch used in Fig. 403.

Plate 46—BLOCKS AND TACKLES

As in any mechanical hookup, there is a certain amount of loss through friction in all tackles. It is difficult to determine the exact amount of friction loss since it is based on many elements, such as: mechanical perfection of the blocks; the relation of rope to sheave; conditions under which the lift is being made, in regard to lead of movable block and hauling part. Engineers have determined that under conditions as nearly perfect as possible, the ratio of power to weight will be as indicated in the table on page 150.

A general rule for determining the power required to raise a given weight with a tackle, is to divide the weight to be raised by the number of parts of rope at the movable block or blocks, the quotient being the power required to produce a balance, friction not considered.

To find the amount of purchase required to raise a given weight with a given power, divide the weight by the power, and the quotient will be the number of parts of rope to be attached to the lower block.

To find the weight a given tackle will raise, multiply the weight a single rope will bear, by the number of parts at the moving block.

When one tackle is put upon another, multiply the two powers together to get the total amount of purchase gained.

Remember that a considerable amount of friction loss must be dealt with, and always make plenty of allowance

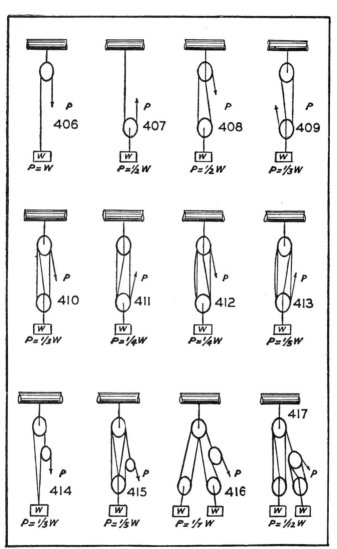

406
$P = W$

407
$P = \frac{1}{2} W$

408
$P = \frac{1}{2} W$

409
$P = \frac{1}{3} W$

410
$P = \frac{1}{3} W$

411
$P = \frac{1}{4} W$

412
$P = \frac{1}{4} W$

413
$P = \frac{1}{5} W$

414
$P = \frac{1}{3} W$

415
$P = \frac{1}{5} W$

416
$P = \frac{1}{7} W$

417
$P = \frac{1}{12} W$

Plate 46—BLOCKS AND TACKLES

when using these rules. Another thing to remember is that power can only be gained at the expense of time.

		Friction not Considered	Friction Considered
Fig. 406:	*Single Whip*	$P = W$	$\dfrac{P}{W} = \dfrac{11}{10}$
Fig. 407:	*Single Whip* with block at weight	$\dfrac{P}{W} = \dfrac{10}{20}$	$\dfrac{P}{W} = \dfrac{12}{20}$
Fig. 408:	*Gun Tackle Purchase*	$\dfrac{P}{W} = \dfrac{10}{20}$	$\dfrac{P}{W} = \dfrac{12}{20}$
Fig. 409:	The same inverted	$\dfrac{P}{W} = \dfrac{10}{30}$	$\dfrac{P}{W} = \dfrac{13}{30}$
Fig. 410:	*Luff Tackle*	$\dfrac{P}{W} = \dfrac{10}{30}$	$\dfrac{P}{W} = \dfrac{13}{30}$
Fig. 411:	The same inverted	$\dfrac{P}{W} = \dfrac{10}{40}$	$\dfrac{P}{W} = \dfrac{14}{40}$
Fig. 412:	*Double Purchase*	$\dfrac{P}{W} = \dfrac{10}{40}$	$\dfrac{P}{W} = \dfrac{14}{40}$
Fig. 413:	The same inverted	$\dfrac{P}{W} = \dfrac{10}{50}$	$\dfrac{P}{W} = \dfrac{15}{50}$
Fig. 414:	*Spanish Burton*	$\dfrac{P}{W} = \dfrac{10}{30}$	$\dfrac{P}{W} = \dfrac{13}{30}$
Fig. 415:	*Double Spanish Burton*	$\dfrac{P}{W} = \dfrac{10}{50}$	$\dfrac{P}{W} = \dfrac{15}{50}$
Fig. 416:	*Bell Purchase*	$\dfrac{P}{W} = \dfrac{10}{70}$	$\dfrac{P}{W} = \dfrac{17}{70}$
Fig. 417:	*Luff upon Luff*	$\dfrac{P}{W} = \dfrac{10}{120}$	$\dfrac{P}{W} = \dfrac{22}{120}$

Plate 47—BLOCKS AND TACKLES

Fig. 418: A *Runner*. Adds an additional power when used with a purchase.

Fig. 419: A *Single Whip*. No power is gained.

Fig. 420: A *Double Whip*. Two times the power is gained.

Fig. 421: A *Gun Tackle*. Two or three times the power is gained, depending upon which is the movable block.

Fig. 422: A *Watch or Single Luff Tackle*. Three times the power is gained.

Fig. 423: A *Double Luff Tackle*. Five times the power is gained.

Fig. 424: A *Two-Fold Purchase*. Four times the power is gained.

Fig. 425: A *Single Spanish Burton*. Three times the power is gained.

Fig. 426: A *Double Spanish Burton*. Five times the power is gained.

Fig. 427: A *Double Spanish Burton* (second method). Five times the power is gained.

Fig. 428: A *Three-Fold Purchase*. Six times the power is gained.

Terminology of Block and Rope Tackle

Bell's Purchase: Four single blocks, two fixed and two movable.

Block: A wooden or metal frame in which are fitted sheaves or pulleys over which rope is led.

Boom tackle: Used to guy out booms on a fore and aft rigged ship while sailing before the wind.

Breech: End of block opposite the swallow.

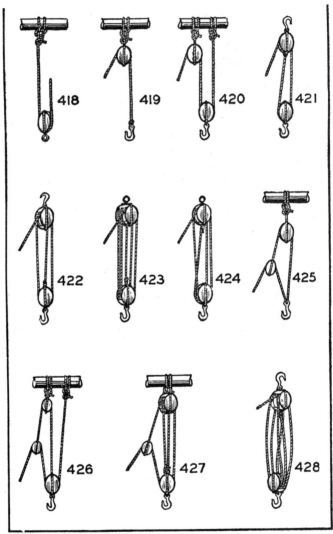

Plate 47—BLOCKS AND TACKLES

Burton: Tackle used for heavy lifts on deck or from the mast, where it is hooked to a pendant near the masthead.

Cheeks: Side pieces on the frame of a block.

Chump block: Egg-shaped block with rounded shell.

Deck tackle: A two-fold heavy purchase used in connection with ground tackle, etc.

Double luff: A double and treble block.

Double Spanish Burton: Three single blocks, or one double and two single blocks.

Fall: That part of a rope tackle to which power is applied for hoisting.

Fiddle block: Same as a sister block except that in the fiddle block the falls lead the same way.

Fish block: Lower block of a fish tackle fitted with a fish hook for fishing an old-fashioned anchor.

Gin block: Shell serving as a guard to hold rope in the score of the sheave.

Gun tackle: Two single blocks.

Handybilly: Small light tackle used for miscellaneous work.

Hatch tackle: Used for hoisting and lowering in hatches.

Hauling part: End of falls to which power is applied.

Jigger: Small light tackle used for a variety of work aboard ship, such as lifting sails up the yards, etc.

Luff or *Watch tackle:* A single and double block with the standing part of the fall fixed to the single block.

Luff upon luff: A luff tackle used in connection with the hauling part of another luff.

Reeve: To pass the rope around the wheel or sheave of a block.

Relieving tackle: Used for the same purpose as the tiller rope in steering. This tackle is rove on the quadrant when there is too much strain on the wheel.

Rolling tackle: Used on quarter of lower yards to relieve strain in heavy weather.

Round in: To bring two blocks together.

Rudder tackle: Used on rudder pendants for emergency.

Runner: A single movable block which supplies additional power to a purchase.

Secret block: Used to prevent fouling.

Sheave: A wheel or pulley over which a rope runs.

Sheet block: Half a shell covering the sheaves.

Single Spanish Burton: Two single blocks and a hook.

Sister block: Two sheaves in one shell, fitted for leading falls in opposite directions.

Snatch block: A single sheave block that is used to give a fair lead to the hauling part of a tackle.

Standing part: That part of the fall made fast to a block.

Stock and bill tackle: Used in bygone days for hauling anchors to and from the billboard.

Swallow: The space between the sheave and frame of the block through which the rope passes.

Tackle: A combination assemblage of ropes and blocks for the purpose of increasing pull or multiplying force.

Three-fold purchase: Two treble blocks.

Thwartship tackle: A term applied to any tackle used for thwartship or across deck.

Topping lift: A rope tackle leading from the masthead of a ship for raising or topping booms.

Two-blocked: Two blocks in close unity.

Two-fold purchase: Two double blocks.

Whip: A single block and rope purchase.

Whip and runner: A whip hooked to the hauling part of a runner.

Yard or stay tackle: Used over a hatch where it is made fast to a stay while hoisting and transferring stores.

TERMINOLOGY

The following names, definitions, and terms apply to the various kinds of ropes and knots and to their applications:

Rope Construction

Rope is made by twisting fibers together into yarns or threads, then twisting the yarns into strands, and finally twisting the strands together to form the finished rope. As the rope is built up, each part successively is twisted in an opposite direction; thus, the yarns are formed with a right-handed twist, the strands are formed with a left-handed twist and the rope is formed with a right-handed twist. This forms a right-handed plain laid rope. If three or more of these right-handed plain laid ropes are used as strands twisted together left-handed to form another rope, it will be a left-handed hawser, or cable-laid rope.

It is customary, when a rope has four or more strands, to put a core or line on the center to retain the rounded form of its exterior; this core or line is called the heart.

Rope is designated as right-laid or left-laid, according to the direction in which the strands are twisted. To determine which way the rope is laid, look along the rope, and if the strands advance to the right, or in a clockwise direction, the rope is right-laid; on the other hand, if the strands advance to the left or in a counterclockwise direction, the rope is left-laid.

Small Cordage

Small cordage: Commonly referred to as small stuff; may mean any small cord or line. However, halyards and other similar lines are not usually referred to as small stuff. Cords are generally designated by the number of threads of which they are made, 24-thread stuff being the largest. Aside from being known by the number of threads, various kinds of small stuff have names of their own, such as:

Spun yarn: This is the cheapest, and is most commonly used for seizings, serving, etc., where neatness is not important. It is laid up loosely, left-handed, in 2, 3, and 4 strands, and is tarred.

Marline: Cord of this kind has the same applications as spun yarn, but it makes a neater job. It is 2-stranded and laid up left-handed. Untarred marline is used for sennit, a braided cord or fabric made from plaited yarns. Tarred yacht marline is used in rigging lofts.

Houseline and *roundline:* These lines are used for the same purpose as marline. They are 3-stranded cord; houseline is laid up left-handed and roundline, right-handed.

Hambroline: This is 3-stranded small stuff, laid up right-handed, and is made of fine, back-handed untarred hemp yarns. It is also called hamberline.

White line or *Cod line:* These lines are small stuff made of untarred American hemp or cotton.

Seizing stuff: This is a heavier line than any of the other small stuff, and it is used when a strong, neat job is required. It is a finished machine-made rope, commonly 3-stranded, of right-handed stuff. There may be 2, 3 or 4 threads to the strand, making 6, 9 or 12 thread seizing stuff. Tarred American hemp is the material used in its manufacture.

Ratline stuff: This is much the same as seizing stuff, except that it is larger. Its sizes usually run from 6 to 24 threads. It is generally 3-stranded line.

Fox: This is comprised of two yarns hand-twisted, or one yarn twisted against its lay and rubbed smooth with the hands against the knee.

156

Rope Materials

Fiber rope: Under this heading are such materials as Manila, hemp, cotton and flax. It takes its name from the species of plant from which the fiber is taken. Fiber rope is impregnated with oil when manufactured, which adds 10% to its actual weight. The oil lengthens the life of the rope by keeping out heat and moisture. As the oil leaves, the rope tends to deteriorate rapidly. The strength of fiber rope decreases with usage and a used rope is often deceptive, because it may not be as serviceable as it looks. Unlike a wire rope, the strands of fiber rope do not wear flat, thereby giving a visible sign of weakness. The fibers may stretch and twist, but this does not always indicate decreased strength. It is not advisable to place a maximum strain on a rope that has been under a load for any considerable length of time, or one that has been strained nearly to the breaking point. The safety of rope decreases rapidly with constant use, depending, of course, upon the circumstances and the amount of strain to which it is subjected.

Abaca, or *Manila rope:* This is the most important cordage fiber in the world today. It possesses a lightness and strength with which no other fiber can compare. Salt or sea water has little effect upon it, and therefore it is used almost exclusively for marine cordage. It is made from the fibers of the abaca plant, and its principal source is Manila, hence its name.

Hemp or *sisal:* The fibers of these plants are used extensively in rope making. The plants grow abundantly in Italy, Russia, the United States and Mexico. Most of the rope used in the United States Navy is made from American hemp, which is equal in quality to that of any of the other countries from which the fibers are obtained. However, hemp rope is little used today, except occasionally

157

for standing rigging, since most of the present-day standing rigging is made of wire rope. When used as rigging it is always tarred. The tar tends to protect it from moisture and increase its life, but decrease its strength.

Coir: Coir is obtained from the fibrous husks of coconuts. Rope made from it is buoyant and does not become waterlogged easily. It has about one-half the strength of Manila rope and finds its chief use in light lines.

Cotton and flax: Both of these materials are employed in rope making although they are used little aboard ship, except as small stuff. The taffrail log, signal halyards and leadlines are made of cotton, while braided flax is used for boat leadlines.

CARE AND HANDLING OF ROPE

Opening a coil of rope may seem very simple, but many a seaman has found himself in "trouble" with a new line, because he did not stop to think before blindly grabbing an end and starting to measure off the amount he wanted. To prevent kinks, first inspect the coil and locate the inside end, which is within the eye. (The eye is the opening in the center of the coil.) Then turn the coil over so that the inside end is down; reach down inside of the eye and take hold of the end and pull it up through the eye; as it comes out it should uncoil counterclockwise.

Rope manufacturers recommend that the lashings around a coil of rope should be cut from the inside of the eye, while the burlap coverings are left on the outside of the coil. Rope shrinks in length when it is wet. If it is held taut in dry weather it will be subjected to great strain when it becomes wet, sometimes so great that it will part. Therefore taut lines should be slacked off when they become wet. Even a heavy dew will penetrate an old line; for this reason, running rigging should be eased off at night.

Both heat and moisture will cause rope to lose its strength. Therefore, rope should always be stored in a cool but dry place. Wet rope should never be stored, nor should it be covered in such a manner that it will retain the moisture it contains. Rope should be covered to protect it from the weather, and it should be parceled to avoid chafing.

Coiling Rope

Straight coil: Lay a bight of the secured end on deck and lay additional bights on top of it, keeping out all kinks and coils, until the entire length of line is laid down. Turn the entire coil over and it will be clear for running.

To *Flemish* down a line, make a small circle of the free end and continue to lay small circles around it until the entire line is down and has the appearance of a coiled clock spring.

To *fake* down a line, lay a short length of the free end out in a straight line, then turn back a loop to form a close flat coil; continue to lay flat coils with the ends on top of the ends of the preceding coil. Always coil a line with the lay.

Right-handed rope should always be coiled "with the sun," that is, in a clockwise direction.

Left-handed rope should always be coiled "against the sun," that is, in a counterclockwise direction.

GLOSSARY

In its true sense, the word "knot" is any fastening made by interweaving rope or cordage, yet in the common sense the term is generic in that it is considered as including many kinds and varieties of actual knots, as well as other rope fastenings such as those known as bends, hitches and splices.

The three principal classes of knots, in the commonly accepted meaning of the term, are:

Bend, from the same root-word as "bind," is defined as a method of joining the ends of two ropes together, or in the language of the sea, the bending of two ropes together, as in the sheet bend, carrick bend, etc.

Hitch is an old English word applied to a method of securing a rope to some object such as a spar (as the clove hitch), or to another rope (as the rolling hitch).

Knot, from the Anglo-Saxon *Cnotta*, refers to a method of forming a knob in a rope by turning the rope on itself through a loop, as exemplified by the overhand knot, the bowline knot, and the running knot.

The use of these three terms of classification in connection with the word "knot" appears to be arbitrary, since there is very little difference between the fisherman's bend and the timber hitch. In one sense, the knot and seizing are considered permanent fastenings which must be unwoven or disentangled in order to be unfastened, while the bend or hitch can be unfastened merely by pulling the ropes in the opposite or reverse direction from that in which they are intended to hold.

There are many other terms used in connection with the tying of knots and with the uses of rope and cordage, most of which are given in the following glossary. This is quite general in its scope and contains many terms which do not apply to knots and rope, but which are closely related to their application.

Knot and Rope Terms

Abaca: A plant which grows chiefly in the Philippine Islands, from which the fibers are taken for making so-called Manila rope. The abaca is similar to a banana plant.

Abaca rope: Rope made from the fibers of the abaca plant; also called Manila rope, since most of the abaca fibers are obtained from that locality.

Against the sun: A nautical term meaning rotation in a counterclockwise, or left-handed direction, in contradistinction to clockwise, or right-handed, as in the direction of rotation of the sun.

Back-handed rope: In rope making the general practice is to spin the yarn over from left to right, or clockwise, making the rope yarn right-handed. The strand formed by a combination of such yarns is given a left-handed twist, and three of these strands are laid up together with an opposite twist to form a right-handed or plain-laid rope.

In making back-handed rope the strands are twisted in the same direction as the yarns. Back-handed rope is more pliable than plain-laid rope and is less likely to kink.

Baseball stitch: A form of stitching or sewing used in sail making and repairing.

Becket: A rope eye for the hook of a block. Also, a rope grommet used as a rowlock, or any small rope strop used as a handle.

Becket bend: An efficient bend used for uniting the two ends of a rope or the end of a rope to an eye. It jams tight with the strain, will not slip, and is easily cast off.

Beeswax: This wax matter, derived from the honeycomb found in beehives, is used extensively in canvas work. It is applied to the sail twine to prevent the small threads from fraying as the twine is pulled through the canvas. It is usually in the form of a wad.

Belay: To make a rope or a line fast by winding it in figure-of-eight fashion around a cleat, a belaying pin, or a pair of bitts. It also means to stop or cease.

Belaying pin: A pin of either wood or metal set in such places as pin rails, etc., upon which to belay a rope or secure the running rigging.

Bend: As defined previously. Also, to secure, tie or make fast, as to bend two ropes together.

Bight: A loop in a rope, as that part of the rope between the end and the standing part, formed by bringing the end of the rope around, near to, or across its own part.

Bitt: One or more heavy pieces of wood or metal, usually set vertically in the deck of a vessel, for the purpose of securing mooring lines and tow lines.

Bitt a cable: To make a line fast by a turn under the thwartship piece and again around the bitt-head; to weather-bitt a cable, an extra turn is taken; to double-bitt is to secure by passing a line around a pair of bitts.

Bitt head: The upper part of a bitt; its head or top.

Bitter-end: The last part of a cable that is doing useful work. In the case of an anchor chain, its bitter-end is made fast in the bottom or side of the chain locker.

Block: A mechanical device consisting essentially of a frame or shell, within which is mounted a sheave or roller over which rope is run. There are many varieties of blocks which are at times called pulleys, or, when rigged, a block and tackle. The name pulley, when applied to a block, is a misnomer, because the pulley is only the sheave or roller, not the whole device.

162

Bollard: A heavy piece of wood or metal set in the deck of a vessel or on the dock to which the mooring lines are made fast. They are also called niggerheads.

Boltrope: A piece of rope sewed into the edge of a piece of canvas or a sail to give added strength and to prevent the canvas from ripping. It is made of hemp or cotton cordage and the name is now applied to a good quality of long-fiber Manila or hemp.

Braid: To plat, plait or interweave strands, yarns, ropes or cords.

Breast line: A mooring line that leads from the breast of a ship to a cleat on the dock, without leading forward or aft.

Bridle: Any span of rope with its ends secured.

Cable: A heavy rope used in attaching anchors or in towing. A cable is also a nautical measure of length. (*See* Cable-length.)

Cable-laid: Cable-laid rope is made of three ropes laid up together left-handed; the individual ropes comprising the strands being laid up right-handed. It is also called hawser-laid rope.

Cable-length: A nautical measure of length. The term was derived originally from the length of a ship's cable, but it now bears no relation to the length of any present-day cable. Many recognized authorities on the subject differ widely in their explanations of the definition of the term. Most of them, however, define a cable length as being equal to 120 fathoms, although in some instances it is given as 100 fathoms. Admiral Luce, in his work on *Seamanship*, published in 1863, gives the most enlightening definition of a cable-length and a plausible reason for it. His explanation is that custom limited the length of cables to 120 fathoms because rope walks of early times were not long enough to lay up strands of greater length. To lay up a cable longer than 120 fathoms,

163

the rope walks would have to be one-third longer than the cable, as this extra length would be needed for drawing down the yarns and laying up the strands. Other difficulties in rope making contributed to limiting the lengths of rope walks, and hence of cables.

Canvas: A woven fabric of cotton or flax used for sails, awnings, and many other shipboard purposes. It is made in varying degrees of weight or quality, numbered from 00, the coarsest, to 10, the finest weave. The term in nautical parlance is synonymous with sail.

Catch a turn: To take a turn, as around a capstan or bitt, usually for holding temporarily.

Caulking: To drive oakum or cotton into the seams of the deck or the ship's side as a means of preventing leakage. Also, the pieces of oakum or cotton used for caulking purposes.

Cavil: A strong timber, bollard, or cleat, used for making fast the heavier lines of a vessel. Also called kevel.

Chafe: To rub or abrade.

Chafing gear: A winding of small stuff, rope, canvas or other materials around spars, rigging, ropes, etc., to prevent chafing.

Chafing mat: A mat made from woven ropes or cordage to prevent chafing.

Clap on: A nautical term with several meanings, as: to seize or take hold of, clap on more sail, and clap a wall or crown on the end of a rope.

Cleat: A heavy piece of wood or metal having two horns around which ropes may be made fast or belayed. Usually secured by bolts or lashings to some fixed object, as the deck of a vessel or the dock.

Clinch: A form of bend consisting of a bight or eye made by seizing the end to its own part. Two kinds of clinches are used, one known as an inside clinch and the other as an outside clinch. A clinch may also be an oval

164

washer, sometimes called a clinch ring, which is used on spikes and bolts when they are employed in wooden construction.

Clockwise: Rotation in the direction of the hands of a clock, or right-handed, in contradistinction to counter-clockwise, or left-handed.

Clothes stop: Small cotton line used for stopping clothes to a line or for securing clothes rolled up in bags or lockers.

Cod line: Small stuff made of 18-thread untarred American hemp or cotton.

Coil: A series of rings, or a spiral, as of rope, cable, etc. Most rope is sold by the coil, which contains 200 fathoms. Also, to lay a rope or cable down in circular turns. If a rope is coiled right-handed, that is, in the direction of rotation of the hands of a clock, it is coiled from left to right, or with the sun. Hemp rope is always coiled in this manner.

Coir: The fibers of the outer husks of the coconut.

Coir rope: Rope made from coir fibers. It is extremely light in weight but is not as strong as rope or cable made from the other common rope materials.

Concluding line: A small rope or line rove through the middle of the steps of a Jacob's ladder.

Cord: Comprised of several yarns, usually cotton or hemp, laid up the opposite way, with an extra twist. Also a term used to distinguish small stuff from rope.

Cordage: A general term now commonly employed to include all ropes and cords, but more specifically, it applies to the smaller cords and lines. Also used as a collective term in speaking of that part of a ship's rigging made up of ropes, etc.

Core: A small rope run through the center of heavier rope. It is usually found in 4-stranded rope, lending it a smooth, round outside appearance

165

Cotton: The fibers of the cotton plant, used in making ropes and small stuff.

Cotton canvas: Fabric made from cotton yarns.

Cotton rope: Rope made from cotton fibers or yarns.

Counterclockwise: Opposite in rotation to the hands of a clock, or left-handed, in contradistinction to right-handed or clockwise.

Cow's tail: Frayed end of rope. The same as dead men and Irish pennant.

Creasing stick: A wood or metal tool, slotted at one end, used for creasing or flattening seams in canvas preparatory to stitching.

Cringle: A piece of rope spliced into an eye over a thimble in the boltrope of a sail.

Cross turns: Turns taken around a rope at right angles to the turns of the lashings or seizing.

Crown: In knotting, to tuck the strands of a rope's end so as to lock them in such a manner as to prevent unraveling by back-splicing the strands. A crown over a wall knot is the first step in tying a manrope knot.

Dead men: The frayed ends of ropes. Same as cow's tail and Irish pennant.

Dead rope: A rope in a tackle not led through a block or sheave.

Earing: A short piece of rope secured to a cringle for the purpose of hauling out the cringle.

Elliott eye: A thimble spliced in the end of a cable or hawser.

End: In knotting, that part of a rope extending from the bight to its extremity, in which the standing part of the rope is on one side of the knot, and the end on the other.

End seizing: A round seizing on the ends of ropes.

Eye: A loop in the end of a rope, usually made permanent by splicing or seizing.

166

Eye seizing: A seizing used for shortening an eye, the turns of the seizing stuff being taken over and under each part, and the ends crossed over the turns.

Fag end: An unraveled or untwisted end of rope, or as applied to flags and pennants, the ragged end.

Fair leader: Lines employed for the purpose of leading other lines in a desired direction. That is, they may be used to pull a line at an angle for the purpose of securing it to a belaying pin or cleat.

Fake: One flat loop or coil of rope which is coiled free for running. Also, to fake down a rope is to coil rope in flat loops so that it is free for running.

Fall: A rope which, with the blocks, makes up a tackle. A fall has both a hauling part and a standing part, the latter being the end secured to the tail of the block. In some cases only the hauling part is considered as the fall.

Fast: Attached or secured to. To make fast means to secure or attach.

Fiber: The smallest thread-like tissue of a rope, cord, or thread, such as the fibers of flax, cotton, hemp, Manila, etc. They are twisted to make the yarn from which the rope is made.

Fiber rope: Rope made from the fibers of abaca, hemp, coir, Manila, sisal, etc.

Fid: A tapered piece of hardwood or a pin, similar in form to a marlinespike and used for the same purpose, such as to separate the strands of a rope for making splices.

Flat seam: The most common method of sewing two pieces of canvas together. The seam is made by lapping the two pieces of canvas, then pushing the needle through the lower piece, and up through the piece to be joined.

Flax: The fibers of the flax plant twisted into yarns for the purpose of making ropes, cords, and small stuff, as well as canvas fabric.

167

Flax canvas: Fabrics made from yarns twisted from flax fibers.

Flax rope: Rope made from yarns twisted from flax fibers.

Flemish coil: There are several versions of the exact meaning of the term. One, that it is a coil in which each fake rides directly on top of the fake below it. Another version is that a Flemish coil, also called a Flemish fake or mat, is one in which each fake lies flat and concentrically, giving the appearance of a rope mat. Common practice is to make a concentric rope mat when ordered to Flemish down a coil, and when the order is given to fake, or fake down, it is the practice to lay down a coil with one fake upon the other, for clear running.

Flemish eye: An eye in which the strands are not interwoven but are separated and bound down securely to the main part with seizing.

Foot rope: A stirrup or strap hanging in a bight beneath a yard in which the men stand when furling or reefing sail.

Fox: As previously explained, two yarns hand-twisted, or one yarn twisted against its lay and rubbed smooth.

Frap: To bind or draw together and secure with rope, as two slack lines.

Frapping turns: Same as cross turns.

Freshen the nip: To shift or secure a rope in another part to minimize wear.

Gantline: A whip or light line made fast aloft for the purpose of hoisting a boatswain's chair or for hoisting sails aloft for bending. Also called girtline.

Garland: A strop used primarily for the purpose of hoisting spars.

Garnet: An arrangement of tackle used to hoist cargo.

Gasket: The term has several nautical meanings. In one sense a gasket is a rope or band of canvas by means of which sails are made fast to the booms or yards. Canvas and sennit bands used to secure a sail are called harbor gaskets, while a rope wound around a sail and a yard arm to the bunt is called a sea gasket. Gaskets are also defined as any kind of packing employed for making joints water- or gas-tight.

Geswarp: A hauling line laid out by a boat, a portion of which is coiled down in the boat. Also called guess warp, or a line for mooring a boat to a boom.

Girtline: Same as gantline.

Gooseneck: A bight made in the standing part of a rope in forming a bowline.

Grab rope: A rope used as a handrail, such as a line secured waist high above a boat-boom or gangplank for steadying one's self.

Graft a rope: To taper the end of a rope and cover it completely with an ornamental arrangement of half hitches of small stuff.

Grafting: To cover a strap, ringbolt, or any similar article with log-line, cord or small stuff.

Grommets: Eyelets made of rope, leather, metal, and other materials. Their chief uses are as eyelets secured to canvas and sails, through which stops or robands are passed.

Guess warp: Same as geswarp.

Guest rope: A grab rope running alongside a vessel to assist boats coming alongside.

Guy: Any rope used for steadying purposes.

Gypsy: The drum of a windlass or winch around which a line is taken for hauling in.

Halyard: Any of the small ropes and tackles used for hoisting sails, flags, etc.

Hamber: Three-strand seizing stuff tight-laid, right-handed. Also called hambroline. It is usually made of un-tarred hemp and is similar to roundline.

Hambroline: Same as hamber.

Hand rope: Same as grab rope.

Hauling line: Usually a line sent down from aloft for the purpose of hauling up gear. Any line used for hauling purposes.

Hauling part: That part of the rope in a tackle which is hauled upon. It might be described as the end of the falls, or a rope to which power is applied.

Hawser: Any large rope, five or more inches in circumference, used principally for kedging, warping and towing.

Hawser-laid: Left-handed rope of nine strands laid up in the form of three 3-stranded, right-handed ropes.

Heart: Same as core.

Heave: To haul or pull on a line, or to cast a heaving line.

Heave taut: To pull tight or stretch.

Heaving line: A light, flexible line having a monkey fist on its free end, the other end being bent to a heavy line. It is heaved ashore or to another vessel as a so-called messenger line, to lead the heavier line, as when it is desired to pass a mooring line to a dock.

Hemp: The fibers of the hemp plant used in making rope. The fibers of this plant are obtained from Italy, Russia, America and other countries. That obtained from New Zealand is called phormium hemp, and that from the East Indies is known by the name of sunn hemp. Rope made of hemp fibers is usually tarred; when untarred, it is called white rope. American hemp is distinguished by its dark gray color.

Hemp rope: Rope made from the fibers of the hemp plant.

Herringbone stitch: A form of stitching or sewing used in sail making and in the sewing of canvas.

Hide rope: Many-ended sisal, used for tying hides.

170

Hitch: As previously explained, or a combination of turns for securing a rope to a spar or stay.

Hook rope: A rope with a hook secured to its end, used for clearing cable chains, etc.

Houseline: Three-stranded cord or small stuff laid up left-handed and used for seizings, etc. Sometimes called roundline, although the latter is laid up right-handed.

Irish pennant: Same as cow's tail and dead men. Also Irish pendant.

Jam: To wedge tight.

Junk: Salvaged rope which is made up into swabs, spun yarn, nettle-stuff, lacings, seizings, earings, etc.; little used today.

Jute: The fibers obtained from East Indian plants, used in making sacking, burlap and twine.

Jute rope: Rope made from jute fibers.

Keckling: Chafing gear applied to a cable, usually made up of old rope.

Kedging: Moving a vessel by alternately laying out a small anchor or kedge and hauling the vessel up to it.

Kevel: Same as cavil. Also spelled kevil.

Kink: A twist in a rope.

Knife: Heavy knives such as those used by sailors form an important part in the working of rope and canvas.

Knittles: Rope yarns twisted and rubbed smooth for pointing and similar purposes. Two or more yarns may be twisted together, or one yarn may be split and its halves twisted. Also called nettles.

Knot: As previously described, refers to a method of turning the rope on itself through a loop.

Lacing: Small rope or cord used to secure canvas or sails by passing it through eyelets in the canvas.

Lang-lay rope: Wire rope in which the individual wires comprising the rope are twisted in the same direction as the strands which make up the rope.

Lanyard: Four-stranded tarred hemp rope, used for making anything fast. Also, an ornamental braid or plait used by sailors in securing their knives, etc.

Lash: To secure by binding with rope or small stuff.

Lashing: A binding or wrapping of small stuff used to secure one object or line to another, as an eye to a spar.

Lashing eye: Loops in the ends of two ropes, through which are passed the lashings which bind them together.

Lasket: Loops of small cord used to lace the bonnet to the jib. Sometimes called latching or latch.

Latching: Same as lasket.

Lay: The direction in which the strands of a rope are twisted. This may be either right-handed (clockwise), or left-handed (counterclockwise). It also refers to the degree of tightness with which the strands are twisted, as soft, medium, common, plain and hard lay. Also used in the expressions "against the lay" and "with the lay," as denoting a direction either opposite to or with the lay of the strands of the rope.

Leading part: Same as hauling part.

Leadline: A line secured to the ship's lead which is used for sounding the depth of water under a vessel. A leadline is made of braided cotton cord for a ship, braided flax for a boat, and hemp for deep sea purposes. These materials are now being replaced with fine wire, wound on reels. (Pronounced led).

Left-handed: Direction of rotation from right to left, counterclockwise or against the sun, in contradistinction to right-handed, clockwise, or with the sun.

Left-handed rope. Rope in which the yarns, strands and rope are laid up exactly the opposite of right-handed rope.

Line: Any rope or line, the word being more commonly used in marine practice than the term "rope."

Log line: A line attached to a ship's log, which is an indicator for measuring speed and distance. The taffrail log line is made of braided cotton twine, while the chip log line is made of hemp.

Loop: Same as a bight.

Man rope: A rope hung over the ship's side for the purpose of ascending or descending. Also, a term used for a handrail on gangways.

Manila: A term used to describe rope made from the abaca fiber, which comes chiefly from the Philippines.

Manila rope: Rope made from the fibers of the abaca; the chief source is Manila or the Philippine Islands.

Marl: To make secure or bind with a series of marline hitches.

Marline: See definition under "Small Cordage."

Marlinespike: A metal pin tapering to a point, used chiefly for splicing wire rope, etc.

Marry: To bind two lines together temporarily, either side by side or end to end.

Match rope: An inflammable rope used as a fuse.

Meshing gauge: A gauge used in making the meshes in nets. It may be of any length to suit the user's convenience, but its width determines the size of the mesh in the net. Thus, a meshing gauge one inch wide will form a mesh one-half inch square.

Meshing needles: Needles such as these are usually made of wood, but many have been made from light metal. They are used in the form of a shuttle for passing the cord and tying knots in the making of nets. It should be understood in winding the cord on the needle, that both the needle and the cord it contains must be small enough to pass through the mesh of the net. They may be made of any desired length.

Messenger line: A light line such as a heaving line used for hauling heavy lines, as from a ship to a dock.

173

Middle a rope: To double a rope in such a manner that the two parts are of equal length.

Mooring line: A line such as a cable or hawser used for mooring a vessel.

Mousing: A short piece of small stuff seized across the opening of the hook of a block as a safety measure.

Nettles: Same as knittles.

Nip: A short turn in a rope. To pinch or close in upon.

Painter: A short piece of rope secured to the bow of a small boat, used for making the boat fast. Not to be confused with sea painter.

Palm: Used as a sailor's thimble. It is comprised of a leather strap worn over the hand, to which is attached a metal plate so placed as to fit into the palm of the sailor's hand. It is used primarily in sewing and mending sails and canvas.

Parbuckle: A form of sling consisting of two ropes passed down a ship's side for the purpose of hauling a cask or similar object in the bight of the ropes; one end of each rope being secured, and the other tended.

Parcel: To protect a rope from the weather by winding strips of canvas or other material around it with the lay, preparatory to serving.

Part: To break.

Pass a lashing: To make the necessary turns to secure a line or an object.

Pass a line: To carry a line to or around something, or reeve through and make fast.

Pass a stopper: To reeve and secure a stopper.

Pay out: To slack off on a line or let it run out.

Payed: Painted, tarred or greased to exclude moisture, as payed rope.

Pendant: A length of rope with a block or thimble secured to its end.

Plain laid: Rope in which three left-handed strands of right-handed yarn are twisted together to form a right-handed or plain laid rope.

Plat: Same as braid and plait.

Plait: Same as braid and plat.

Pointing: Any of numerous methods by which the end of a rope is worked into a stiff, cone-shaped point.

Pricker: A light piece of metal, similar to a marlinespike, but having a handle; used for the same purposes as a marlinespike.

Quilting: Any covering of woven ropes or sennit, placed on the outside of a container used for water.

Rack: To seize two ropes together with cross turns of spun yarn or small stuff.

Rack seizing: Small stuff rove around two lines in an over and under figure-of-eight fashion.

Ratline: As previously described, three-stranded, right-handed tarred small stuff, larger than seizing stuff. Also short lines of ratline stuff, run horizontally across shrouds as steps.

Reef: To take in sail, to reduce the effective area of a sail.

Reef cringle: A rope grommet worked into a thimble attached to a sail.

Reef earing: A short length of small stuff spliced into a reef cringle for the purpose of lashing the cringle to a boom or yard.

Reef points: Short pieces of small stuff set in the reef bands of sails for reefing purposes.

Reeve: To pass the end of a rope through an eye or an opening such as a block, thimble, or bight.

Render: To pass through freely. Said of a rope when it runs easily through a fairlead or a sheave.

Riders: A second layer of turns placed over the first layer of turns of a seizing.

175

Riding chock: Chock over which the anchor chain passes.

Riding turns: Same as riders.

Rigging: A term applied to a ship's ropes in general.

Right-handed: Direction of rotation from left to right (clockwise or with the sun), in contradistinction to left-handed (counterclockwise or against the sun).

Right-handed rope: Same as plain laid rope.

Robands: Short pieces of small stuff of Manila or spun yarn, used to secure the luff of a sail. Also called rope bands.

Rogue's yarn: Colored yarn worked into the strands of a rope as an identification mark, and as protection against theft.

Rope: A general term used to describe any cord more than one inch in circumference. All rope was at one time measured by its circumference, except that used for power transmission, which was measured by its diameter. Today, however, rope is usually measured in terms of its diameter.

Rope band: Same as roband.

Roping needle: Short spur needle used for sewing bolt-ropes and for other heavy work.

Roping twine: Nine- to eleven-ply small stuff.

Roping yarn: Untwisted strands of a rope used for rough seizings.

Round seam: A seam employed in sewing canvas and sails. It is used to join two edges by holding them together and passing the needle through them at right angles to the canvas.

Round seizing: A method of securing two ropes together, or the parts of the same rope to form an eye.

Round turn: Passing a line completely around a spar, bitt or another rope.

Rounding: Serving a rope to prevent chafing.

Roundline: Three-stranded cord or small stuff laid up right-handed. Also called houseline, although the latter is laid up left-handed.

Rouse: To heave on a line.

Rubber: A flat steel tool used for rubbing or smoothing down seams in canvas. It is fitted with a wooden handle.

Rumbowline: Coarse soft rope made from outside fibers and yarns and used for temporary lashings, etc.

Running line: Any line, such as a messenger line, which may be used to run out for the purpose of paying out a hawser or cable.

Running rigging: All the lines of a ship used to control the sails.

Sail: Generally, canvas used aboard ship in the form of sails.

Sail hook: A metal hook secured to a small line, used for holding sails and canvas while sewing seams, etc.

Sail needle: Long spur steel needles, triangular at the point and cylindrical at the eye. There are two types, known respectively as sewing and roping needles, and these are in turn called short and long spur needles. Sewing needles come in sizes 6 to 14 and in half-sizes to $17\frac{1}{2}$. Size 15, which is $2\frac{1}{2}$ inches long, is used the most.

Sail twine: Small stuff in the form of thread, made of either cotton or flax. It is available in several different sizes, usually wound into the form of a ball.

Scissors: These are essential in canvas and fancy rope work.

Sea painter: A long rope, not less than $2\frac{3}{4}$ inches in circumference, for use in a ship's lifeboats.

Secure: To attach, fasten or make fast.

Secured end: The part of a line which is attached or secured to an object.

Seize: To put on or clap on a seizing. That is, to bind

with small stuff, as one rope to another, a rope to a spar, etc. Seizings are named from their appearance or from the functions they serve, as throat seizing, flat and round seizings, and others.

Seizing stuff: Small stuff.

Selvage: A border woven in fabric, or the edge of the fabric closed by complicating the threads so as to prevent raveling.

Selvagee: Rope yarn, spun yarn or small stuff marled together and used for stoppers, straps, etc.

Sennit: Braided cordage such as nettles or small stuff, usually of ornamental design. The different kinds are known by many different names, according to their design.

Serving: The process of winding small stuff about a rope or wire, after worming and parceling, the turns being kept very close together to make the end of the rope impervious to water after being tarred. The turns of the serving are made against the lay of the rope. Also called service.

Serving board: A small flat board having a handle, used with a serving mallet for serving rope. The mallet is a typical round, wooden maul with a groove cut lengthwise in its head. Their purpose is to keep the serving taut and the turns close together.

Shakings: Odds and ends of rope and scrap rope which are handpicked into fibers for use as oakum.

Sheave: The roller of a tackle block.

Shoemaker's stitch: A sewing stitch used in making and mending sails and in sewing canvas and other fabrics.

Shroud-laid: Four-stranded rope laid up right-handed.

Shrouds: Ropes of hemp or wire used as side stays from the masthead to the rail.

Sisal: Fibers of the henequin plant which grows abundantly in Yucatan.

Sisal rope: Rope made from fibers of the sisal plant.

Slack: That part of a rope, secured at both ends, which is hanging loose; the opposite of taut.

Sling: To sling a piece of cargo, such as a barrel, by passing a line around it. Or, a sling may be an arrangement of short pieces of rope or chain used for hoisting cargo and other similar purposes. The rope sling or strap is the most common of these. A rope sling is made of short pieces of rope spliced together. It is passed around a cask, for instance, and one bight, the rove, is passed through the other, which is known as the bite. The cargo hook is attached in the rove. Other types of slings are known by such names as web, chain, platform, net, bale, butt, etc.

Small cordage: As previously described; small stuff which may be 1¾ inches in circumference or less.

Spanish fox: Untwisted rope yarn retwisted in the opposite direction.

Spar: A yard, mast, gaff, or boom.

Splice: To join the ends of ropes together, or the end of a rope to its standing part, as in forming an eye, by interweaving the strands of the rope. Splices are known as long, short, chain, sailmaker's, etc.

Spun yarn: Two-, 3- and 4-stranded rough stuff twisted loosely together and laid up left-handed for use as small stuff, especially when a smooth service is desired.

Standing part: In knotting, the standing part of a line is that part of the main rope as distinguished from the bight and the end.

Standing rigging: That part of a ship's rigging used to support its spars which is not altered with the ordinary working of the ship.

Stay: A piece of rigging; usually a rope of hemp or wire used as a support for a mast.

Stop: To seize or lash, usually temporarily.

Stopper: A short line, one end of which is secured to some fixed object, used to check or stop a running line.

Strand: Part of a rope, made up of yarns, the twist of the strand usually being opposite to that of the yarns, except in back-handed rope.

Stranded: A rope is said to be stranded when a strand parts.

Strap: A form of sling, usually employed for handling cargo. Also called a strop. Permanent straps are spliced into the thimble with the hook of a tackle block. A sail strap is one in which the eye is made by a seizing and the bight is tucked through the eye instead of the strap itself.

Strop: Same as strap.

Tackle: An arrangement of ropes and blocks, sometimes called block and tackle. Also pronounced tay-kle. Tackle is employed primarily for hoisting purposes.

Tackline: A short length of line, usually signal halyard, used for separating strings of signals.

Take a turn: To pass a line around a cleat or belaying pin.

Tapered rope: Rope used in places where most of the strain is taken by one end only. The part which bears the strain is full-sized while the remainder of the line tapers off to the hauling part, which is usually light and pliable.

Tarred fittings: Small stuff.

Taut: Tight; the opposite of loose or slack.

Tend: To man or attend.

Thimble: A grooved piece of metal, either circular or heart-shaped, used to receive the eye of a rope.

Thread: Yarn or small stuff made into strands. Small rope or cord is often designated by the number of threads or yarns it contains, as 6-thread seizing stuff.

Throat seizing: A seizing used to lash an eye in a rope,

to hold it around a thimble, or to seize two parts of rope together at the point where they cross.

Thrum mats: Small pieces of canvas with short pieces of rope sewed to them by a method called thrumming. They are used between the rowlocks and the oars to prevent noise.

Thrums: Short pieces of small stuff, secured by their bights to pieces of canvas for use as chafing gear. The verb "thrum" means to attach the small stuff.

Tie: That part of a halyard which hoists a yard. Also, to make a knot.

Tiller rope: Wire rope made of copper, bronze and galvanized wire, laid up left-handed.

Timenoguy: A short piece of rope with a bull's-eye spliced in its end, employed as an intermediate support or guy for stays.

Toggle: A small wooden pin made of hardwood which is inserted into a knot to make it more secure or to make it more readily and quickly unfastened.

Tow line: A cable or hawser used for towing.

Trailing line: A small line attached to the gunwale of a small boat and around the loom of the oars to prevent them from falling overboard when they are trailed.

Trice: To haul up or pull taut.

Tricing line: Any small line used for suspending articles.

Turn: A single winding of rope, as around a bollard or cleat.

Twice-laid rope: Rope made from second-hand rope yarns or strands.

Unbend: To cast off or adrift, let loose or free; to untie.

Unlay: To separate the strands of a rope.

Unreeve: The opposite of reeve.

Veer: To let a rope or chain run out or slack off.

Veer and haul: To slack off and pull alternately.

Warp: To maneuver a ship, as at a dock.

Wheel rope: Rope connecting the steering wheel with the drum of the steering gear. It is composed of six strands and a heart, making seven strands in all.

Whip: To lash the end of a rope to prevent it from fraying. Also used to designate different kinds and arrangements of blocks and tackles, as single whip, double whip, etc.

Whip upon whip: One lashing over the top of the other.

Whipping: The lashing on the end of a rope, or the small stuff used for whipping.

White line: Small stuff made of untarred hemp or cotton.

With the sun: Rotation in the direction of that of the sun, clockwise, or right-handed, in contradistinction to against the sun, counterclockwise, or left-handed.

Worming: Filling up the lays of a rope with spiral windings of small stuff preparatory to parceling, in order to make a round, smooth surface.

Yarn: Any number of threads or fibers twisted together from the various fibers of which rope and cords are made.

Yoke lanyard: A small line rove through or secured to the ends of a yoke.

INDEX OF KNOTS

Bags
sea, 141
Belaying
eye spliced line, 127
halyard to a cleat, 127
line to a belaying pin, 127
making an eye fast to a belaying pin, 128
Bends
anchor, 8
becket, left-handed, 19
—right-handed, 19
—triple, 19
binder twine, 80
bowline splicing, 20
carrick, double, 19
—half, 20
fisherman's, 8
haywire, 91
marriage, single, 19
mogul, 8
prolonged, 20
reeving line, 19
sheet, left-handed, 19
—right-handed, 19
—with toggle, 80
slip, 19
studding-sail tack, 83
toggle, 80

topsail halyard, 11
Blocks and Tackles
bell purchase, 150
gun tackle, 151
luff tackle, 150
—double, 151
—inverted, 150
luff upon luff, 150
purchase, double, 150
—double, inverted, 150
—gun tackle, 150
—gun tackle, inverted, 150
—two-fold, 151
—three-fold, 151
runner, 151
Spanish burton, 150
—single, 151
—double, 150, 151
watch, 151
whip, single, 150, 151
—double, 151
Bowlines
anchor, 115
common, 22
false, 92
French, 22
heaving line, 125
on the bight, 25
—single, 92

183

Bowlines (cont.)
  Portuguese, 25
  ring, 24
  running, 91
  Spanish, 24
  stopper, 24
  water, 89
Braids
  buglers, 91
  chain, 91
  —figure-of-eight, 91
  Higginbotham, 91
  twist, 106
Breaking Twine with Fingers,
  92

Canvas Work
  handworked eyelets, 145
  sea bag, 141
  sewing bolt rope to a sail
    or awning, 147
Chairs
  climber's or pruner's sad-
    dle, 89
  rigging for a boatswain's,
    119
Clews
  attaching clew bights to a
    jackstay, 140
  hammock, 138
Clinches
  inside, 78
  outside, 77
Coachwhipping
  four-strand, 117
Coils
  coiling down rope, 105
  flemishing down rope, 103

heaving line or sash cord,
  105
making up a gasket, 103
overlapping figure-of-eight,
  105
Coxcombs
  three-strand, 115
Cringles
  around a thimble, 144
Crowns
  three-strand, 55

Eyes
  artificial or spindle, 133
  hogs, 94

Fastenings
  single chain, 123
Fenders
  closed hitching, 117
  —open, 117
  —spiral, 119

Gaskets
  making up, 103
Grommets
  hemp laid long spliced, 71
  three-strand, 71

Halters
  adjustable, 70
  hackamore tie, 94
Hammock Making, 137
Hawsers
  faking down, 106
  placing over a bollard, 123
  securing a mooring line, 124

184

securing on a bollard with
  a round turn, 123
three on one bollard, 123
Hitches
belaying pin, 95
bill, 87
binder, 98
Blackwall, single, 87
—double, 87
brickmason's, 114
bulkhead, 103
buntline, 83
—with round turn, 83
buoy, 6
butcher's, 87
cable, 97
camper's, 49
carpenter's, 83
cement worker's, 114
clove, 9
—mooring, 124
—on the standing part, 3
—reverse on the standing
  part, 3
—slip, 12
coil, 103
cow, 3
drayman's, 50
fire hose, 82
fireman's, 82
flag, 87
grocer's, 80
half, single, 3
hammock, 11
handcuff, 44
hoisting, 85
killick, 9
lark's head mooring, 124

lifting, 15
lobster buoy, 83
lone jack diamond, 102
lumber, 102
magnus, 19
marline, 11
marlinespike, 97
messenger's, 97
midshipman's, 5, 97, 114
old-time bedding, 102
packer's, 94
painter's, 89
pin, 95
plumb bob, 92
purlin, 95
racking, 87, 95
Ralph, 49
ranger, 102
ratline, 9
reef pennant, 11
regular stopper, 13
rigger's, 47
ring, 8
rolling, inside, 12
—outside, 12
roofer's, 33
rope coil, 103
round turn mooring, 124
scaffold, 85
shank, 87
simple rope coil, 103
skidder's, 95
slip halter, 12
slippery, 29, 124
stakeman's, 95
storm, 82
stunner, 87
teamster's, 47

Hitches (cont.)
telegraph, 128
temporary, 95
tent stake, 82
timber, 9
trapper's, 49
—with bow, 49
truckman's, 50
true diamond, 102
two half, 3
Waldo, 87
weaver's, 15
well digger's, 97
well pipe, 15
Hitching
closed fender, 117
—open, 117
—spiral, 119

Knots
artillery, 47
bag, 83
bell ringer's, 94
blood, 85
—two-fold, 44
—three-fold, 44
—four-fold, 44
boat, 8
bread bag, 88
brief, 42
bullion, 44
capstan, 5
carrick diamond, two-strand, 29
—double, 31
cat's paw, 95, 97
Chinese button, 89
Chinese temple, two-leaf, 40

—three-leaf, 42
conjurer's, 35
crabber's eye, 35
crossed running, 27
crown, three-strand, 55
Davenport brothers trick, 45
delay, 6
diamond, single, three-strand, 58
—double, 58
—footrope, 106
dragon fly, two-leaf, 39
—three-leaf, 40
draw, 34
Dutchman's, 50
electrician's, 82
figure-of-eight, 27
—double, 44
—running, 27
—three-fold, 44
—trick, 45
fireman's rescue, 108
fisherman's, single, 35
florist's, 80
four-fold, 31
granny, 28
grass, 44
gunner's, 6
hackamore, 29
heaving line, 34
honda, 45
Indian bridle, 29
Japanese, 33
—crown, 37
jury mast, 33
—single, 31
—double, 31

ladder rung, 109
lanyard, three-strand, 55
life boat, 34
lineman's, 45
longshoreman's, 108
man-harness, 47
manrope, single, 57
—double, 57
manifold, 44
marten, 83
mast head, 33
Matthew Walker, three-strand, 58
mattress maker's, 47
miller's, 83
openhand eye, 27
overhand, 27
—running, 27
pitcher, double, 33
pommel, 97
prolong, 6
reef, 28
sack, 83, 85
sennit, three-strand, 59
shamrock, 34
slip, 34
Spanish, 31
square, 28
star, three-strand, 61
stationer's, 102
stevedore's, 25
stopper, single, three-strand, 57
—double, 57
—multiple overhand, 34
—sail twine, 89
strap, 44
surgeon's, 47

terminal, 33
Theodore, 29
thief, 88
three-fold, 31
thumb, 27
tom fool's, 35
trick chain of overhands, 111
underwriter's, 82
wake, 40
wall, 55
weaver's, 45
Knotting a Rope Yarn, 98

Ladders
common rope, 109
stern, 109
Lark's Heads
crossed, 3
double, 5
stoppered, 3
treble, 5
with toggle, 8
Lashings
chain, double, 128
crossed, 130
loop, 130
pole, 128
putlog, 128
rose, 114, 121
shear head, 130
square, 130
wedding, 121
Loops
binder's, 27
farmer's, 50
—second method, 50

Mats
Chinese square, 35
Napoleon bend, 39
paunch, 113
Queen Anne, 39
—double, 40
square, 39
sword, 113
triangle, 37
wrought, 113
Monkey Fists
crowned, 118
three-strand, 118
Mooring Lines
securing, 124
Mousing a Hook, 87

Nets
fish, 135
rope cargo, 134
Nooses
running, 29

Ornamental Designs
Chinese temple, two-leaf, 40
—three-leaf, 42
dragon fly, two-leaf, 39
—three-leaf, 40
sailor's breastplate, 28

Parceling, 113
Pointing
common, 130
ordinary eye, 131
ordinary rope, 133
Poles Lashed and Wedged, 128

Rattling Down, 115
Rope Tools
a fid, 138
a palm, 138

Seizings
becket, 49
clinch, inside, 78
—outside, 77
flat, 78
French, 79
grapevine, 79
middle, 79
necklace, 79
nippered, 79
round, 78
Sennits
crabber's eye, five-strand, 53
English, four-strand, 51
—five-strand, 51
flat single, four-strand, 51
—five-strand, 51
French, seven-strand, 51
—nine-strand, 53
half-round, six-strand, 54
railway, 85
round, four-strand, 51
—six-strand, 54
running, five-strand, 53
square, eight-strand, 54
three-strand, 50
—double, 51
Serving, 113
Sheepshanks
cat shank, 20
cut, 49
—with Spanish knot, 49

dog shank, 20
interlaced, 22
knotted, 20
man o' war, 20
marline hitched, 22
ordinary, 20
sheet bend, 20
with ends double-hitched, 22
with the middle crossed, 22
with toggle, 80
Shortenings
halter, 106
overhand, 22
seized loop, 22
Shroud Knots
American, 109
wall, 109
Slings
bale, 121
butt, 98
cask, 98
Dutch, 100
edge plank, 85
hogshead, 100
horizontal barrel, 98
jug, 94
parbuckle, 98
stage, 124
vertical barrel, 98
Sling Shorteners
regular, 106, 108
Snaking, 77
Spanish Windlass, 111
Splices
back, three-strand, 62
—sailmaker's, 63

chain, 69
cut, 65
eye, three-strand, 63
—four-strand, 65
—Flemish, 133
—round thimble with ends frayed, 65
—sailmaker's, 63
—served, 65
horseshoe, 70
in standing part of rope, 106
long, three-strand, 68
short, three-strand, 67
—sailmaker's, 67
Stitches
baseball, 148
flat, 147
—on a round patch, 148
herringbone, 147
round, 147
Stoppers
common, 127
Strops
selvagee, 121

Taking a Rope Yarn out of a Strand, 111
Ties
becket, double, 44
bosun's knot and half hitch, 100
fisherman's knot, 82
fishhook, 82
game carrier's, 92
hackamore, 6
—halter, 94
halter, 6

Ties (cont.)
  latigo, 6
  manger, 6
  package, 100
  —four-strand, 102
  packer's ligature, 100
Toggles
  bend, 80
  figure-of-eight, 8
  lark's head, 8
  —with sheepshank, 80
  —with sheet bend, 80
Tricing in Two Ropes, 118
Turk's Heads
  three-strand, 15
  —inverted, 40
  four-strand, 16

  five-strand, 17
Walls
  three-strand, 55
Whippings
  American, 73
  French, 75
  grapevine, 75
  herringbone, 77
  ordinary, 74
  palm and needle, 74
  plain, 73
  —in the middle of a line, 74
  sailmaker's, 77
  seaman's, 75
  temporary, 73
Worming, Parceling and Serving. 113

INDEX OF KNOTS BY JOB AND HOBBY

Artillerymen
artillery knot, 47
delay knot, 6
gunner's knot, 6
man-harness knot, 47
prolong knot, 6

Brickmasons
brickmason's hitch, 114
cement worker's hitch, 114
Butchers
butcher's hitch, 77

Campers
camper's hitch, 50
tent stake hitch, 82
tent stake or storm hitch, 82
Carpenters
carpenter's hitch, 83
lumber hitch, 102
Circus Men
tent stake hitch, 82
tent stake or storm hitch, 102
Cowboys
hackamore halter tie, 94
hackamore knot, 29
hackamore tie, 6
halter shortening, 106
halter tie, 6
honda, 45
hondo, 45
latigo tie,

manger tie, 6
pommel knot, 97
slip halter hitch, 12
Theodore knot, 29

Divers
diver's life line knot, 108
fireman's rescue knot, 108
Draymen
drayman's hitch, 50
Dutchman's knot, 50
truckman's hitch, 50

Electricians
electrician's knot, 82

Farmers
adjustable halter, 70
binder twine bend, 80
blocks, tackles, 150-51
farmer's loop, 50
farmer's loop, second method, 50
grass knot, 44
halter shortening, 106
haywire bend, 91
jug sling, 94
strap knot, 44
Firemen
fire hose hitch, 82
fireman's hitch, 82
Fishermen
fisherman's bend, 8

fisherman's knot tie, 82
fishhook ties, 82
fishhook tie, second
     method, 82
single fisherman's knot, 35
Florists
florist's knot, 80
Forest Rangers
ranger's hitch, 102

Grocers
grocer's hitch, 80

Hammock Makers
attaching bights to jackstay,
     140
hammock clews, 138
meshing, 137
Hoisters
hoisting hitch, 85
hoisting hitch, second
     method, 85
killick hitch, 9
purlin hitch, 95
telegraph hitch, 128
Horsemen
grass knot, 44
hackamore knot, 29
hackamore tie, 6
halter shortening, 106
halter tie, 6
Indian bridle, 29
latigo tie, 6
manger tie, 6
slip halter hitch, 12
strop knot, 44
Theodore knot, 29
Hunters
game carrier's tie, 92

Ladder Makers
ladder rung knot, 109
rope ladder, 109
stern rope ladder, 109
Linemen
cable hitch, 97
lineman's knot, 45
messenger hitch, 97
Loggers
killick hitch, 9
poles lashed and wedged,
     128
putlog lashing, 128
skidder's hitch, 95
Longshoremen
longshoreman's knot, 108
regular sling shortener, 106
regular sling shortener, sec-
     ond method, 108
Lumberjacks
killick hitch, 9
poles lashed and wedged,
     128
putlog lashing, 128
timber hitch, 9

Magicians
Arizona handcuff hitches,
     35
Davenport brothers trick
     knot, 45
figure-of-eight trick knot,
     45
tom fool's knot, 35
trick chain of overhand
     knots, 111
Mat Makers
Chinese square mat, 35

Napoleon bend mat weave, 37
paunch mat, 113
Queen Anne mat, 39
Queen Anne mat, doubled, 40
sword mat, 113
triangle mat, 113
wrought, 113
Mattress Makers
mattress maker's knot, 47
Millers
bag knot, 83
binder hitch, **98**
blood knot, 85
miller's knot, 83
sack knot, 85
sack knot, second method, 85
Mountain Climbers
lineman's knot, 45

Net Makers
fish net, 135
rope cargo net, 134

Ornamentalists
brief knot, 42
five-strand Turk's head, 17
four-strand Turk's head, 16
Japanese crown knot, 37
Japanese knot, 33
shamrock knot, 34
success knot, 37
three-leaf Chinese temple knot, 42
three-leaf dragonfly knot, 40

three-strand inverted Turk's head, 40
three-strand Turk's head, 15
two-leaf Chinese temple knot, 40
two-leaf dragonfly knot, 39
two-strand carrick diamond knot, 29
two-strand carrick diamond knot, double, 31
wake knot, 40

Packers and Pack Mule Transportation
four-strand package tie, 102
lone jack diamond, 102
old-time bedding hitch, 102
packer's hitch, 94
packer's ligature, 100
packer's tie, 100
ranger hitch, 102
true diamond hitch, 102
Painters
painter's hitch, 89
roofer's hitch, 33
Power Boatmen
Useful knots will be found on almost every page.
Prospectors
camper's hitch, 50
lone jack diamond, 102
old-time bedding hitch, 102
ranger hitch, 102
tent stake hitch, 82
tent stake or storm hitch, 82
true diamond hitch, 102

Riggers
blocks and tackles, 150, 151
edge plank sling, 85
rigger's hitch, 47
scaffold sling, 85
Roofers
roofer's hitch, 33

Seamen and Sea Scouts
Useful knots will be found
on almost every page.
Sennit Braiders
sennit braids, 50, 51, 53, 54,
91
Shipping Clerks
bosun's knot and half hitch
package tie, 100
four-strand package tie, 102
package tie, 100
running noose, 29
Sling Makers
butt sling, 98
cask sling, 98
Dutch sling, 100
hogshead sling, 100
horizontal barrel sling, 98
parbuckle, 98
vertical barrel sling, 98
Soldiers
see *Artillerymen*
Stationers
running noose, 29
slippery hitch, 29
stationer's knot, 102
Stevedores
regular sling shortener, 106
regular sling shortener, second method, 108
stevedore's knot, 25

stevedore's knot with toggle, 8
Steeplejacks
climber's or pruner's saddle, 89
rigging for a boatswain's
chair, 119
Surgeons
surgeon's knot, 47
Surveyors
plumb bob hitch, 92
stakeman's hitch, 95

Tailors
Chinese button knot, 89
Teamsters
teamster's hitch, 47
Trappers
trapper's hitch, 49
—with bow, 49
Tree Surgeons
climber's   or   pruner's
saddle, 89
Truckmen
drayman's hitch, 50
Dutchman's knot, 50
truckman's hitch, 50
Tugboatmen
Useful knots will be found
on almost every page.

Weavers
weaver's knot, 45
Well Diggers
well digger's hitch, 97

Yachtsmen
Useful knots will be found
on almost every page.